ASSET S
MANAGEMENT
ASM$_x$

A LEADER'S GUIDE TO RELIABILITY TRANSFORMATION IN THE DIGITAL AGE

Jason Apps

ASSET STRATEGY MANAGEMENT ASM_x

A Leader's Guide to Reliability Transformation
in the Digital Age

Jason Apps

ISBN 978-1-941872-87-1
HF012019

© 2018-2019, Reliabilityweb.com and its affiliates.
All rights reserved.

Printed in the United States of America.
This book, or any parts thereof, may not be reproduced, stored in a retrieval system, or transmitted in any form without the permission of the Publisher.
Opinions expressed in this book are solely the author's and do not necessarily reflect the views of the Publisher.

Publisher: Reliabilityweb.com
Design and Layout: Alex Cardoso

For information: Reliabilityweb.com
www.reliabilityweb.com
8991 Daniels Center Drive, Suite 105, Ft. Myers, FL 33912
Toll Free: 888-575-1245 | Phone: 239-333-2500
E-mail: crm@reliabilityweb.com

10 9 8 7 6 5 4 3 2

To deliver real value, it's got to work in your organization

Over 80% of organizations have no formal structure around managing the reliability strategies they are executing.
&
Without governance and control of your reliability strategies, you cannot have governance and control of your assets.

ASSET: An item, thing, or entity that has potential or actual value to an organization

STRATEGY: A plan of action designed to achieve a long-term or overall aim

MANAGEMENT: The process of dealing with or controlling things

ASM
dealing with and controlling the plan of action to achieve your long-term aim through your assets

Table of Contents

Preface viii
Terms and Definitions ix
Introduction xvii
    The business case xviii
    The problem xix
    Driving culture with process and triggers xx
Section 1: A Typical Reliability Environment 1
    Any given site 2
    The focus 6
    The outcome 6
Section 2: The Opportunity 13
Section 3: Work Execution Management (WEM) 19
    What is WEM? 20
    What does WEM deliver? 21
    Limitations of WEM 22
Section 4: Setting a Reliability Strategy 25
    Definition 25
    Routine maintenance and corrective action plans 26
    Asset and/or fleet level decisions 26
    Portfolio level decisions 27
    Value 28
    Methodologies 29
        RCM and variants 30
        Preventive maintenance optimization (PMO) 32
        Maintenance task analysis (MTA) 33
    So which methodology works? 34
Section 5: Setting a Reliability Strategy – Fundamental Concepts 35
    Functional based 36
    Failure mode to task connection 39

The three characteristics of failure 41
Random activity 45
Age related behavior 46
Impacts of failure 47
Maintenance task options 49
Preventive tasks 50
Predictive maintenance 51
Quantitative evaluation 54
Common traps 54
    Mean time between failures (MTBF) 55
    P-F interval 57
Implementation 60

Section 6: Asset Strategy Management (ASM) 63
Key elements to establish ASM 64
Implement a management of change process
for reliability strategy related content 64
Implement a management system and process
for reliability strategy content 66
Implement reliability strategy review triggers 67
Enable rapid deployment of reliability strategy updates 69
The three phases of ASM 71
Build 72
Deploy 73
    Using baseline reliability strategies 74
    Packaging and generating master data 75
    Master data keys 75
    Forecasting reliability strategy performance 76
Governance 77
    Continuous improvement 77
    Compliance 78

Section 7: ASM and Asset Performance Management (APM) .. 81
What is APM? 81

  ASM and APM – Which comes first? 84
  Delivering performance with WEM, APM and ASM 84
Section 8: ASM and Big Data, Digital Transformation
and IIoT 89
  Digital transformation in asset management 89
  Where's the big data? 92
  What can big data really do for you? 92
    Reliability strategy review 92
    Triggering reliability strategy review 93
  ASM and big data 94
  Going digital with ASM 94
Section 9: ASM, Asset Management Systems and
the Uptime Elements 97
Section 10: ASMx – Connected Digital
Reliability Strategies 101
  Consolidating data 102
  Managing variations 104
    Group variations 105
    Local variations 106
    What's not a variation 106
  Variation reporting 107
  Task packaging into work plans 107
  Workflows 108
  ASM process triggers 109
  Leveraging value with ASMx 109
    Productivity 110
    Leveraging key learnings 110
Section 11: ASM and Reliability Culture 113
  What is a reliability culture? 113
  Establishing a reliability culture 114
  Developing a purpose 115
  Leadership education 116

    Implementing ASM 116
    Reliability education 116
    Process education 117
    Measurement 117
    Communicate, communicate, communicate 118
Section 12: Implementing ASMx 119
    Process blueprinting... 120
    Technical solution selection.. 121
    Establish a process 122
    Engagement.. 123
    Support 124
Section 13: ASM and New Projects.. 125
    Reliability studies for new projects... 125
    Build a reliability strategy.. 127
        Deploy.. 127
    Do the reliability strategies deliver the performance?............ 128
Section 14: ASM and RCA 131
    Typical approaches... 131
    Incorporating RCA into ASM 132
    ASM specialists 133
Section 15: ASMx Quick Start 135
    Key elements of a reliability strategy build/review 136
    Baseline reliability strategies 136
    Initial deployment to assets 137
    Implementing a reliability strategy... 138
    ASMx triggers 138
    ASMx technology 139
    ASMx implementation on mature sites 140
Section 16: ASMx – Manage Reliability Strategy
& Drive Performance 143
References 145
About the Author.. 147

Preface

This book describes the asset strategy management (ASM) process, why it's needed and the value it delivers. The fundamental elements of ASM are to build, deploy and then govern and manage asset reliability strategy over the life of an asset.

An asset reliability strategy should be aligned with the performance requirements for the assets and deliver the desired balance of cost risk and performance.

The key concepts of building, deploying and managing asset reliability strategies are covered in some detail, since the effectiveness of any reliability strategy is based on the decision-making process that derives it.

Several statistics noted throughout the book are the result of research conducted via a detailed survey covering over one hundred and fifty organizations spanning most industry verticals.

Section 15 provides a summary of the key elements to build, deploy and govern a sound reliability strategy and begin the journey of implementing ASM from a practical perspective. Experienced reliability practitioners or those who just want to know what direction to begin implementing ASM can read this section on its own. The rest of the book covers the business case, the definition of ASM, details of the key elements of setting a reliability strategy, the key pillars of ASM and how ASM fits into a broader asset management function.

Terms and Definitions

The content of this book aligns with accepted technical definitions, particularly those provided by the International Organization for Standardization (ISO).

However, the following terms and definitions represent simplified, practical definitions, with the purpose of helping readers understand the common terminology used in this book and relate those terms to their accepted definitions.

All the terms and definitions are related to the asset management discipline and, specifically, this book's content.

Asset Investment Planning (AIP)
A process of valuing all potential investments on a common scale and then optimizing the investment portfolio to provide maximum value given the constraints in place (typically financial and resource constraints)
Asset Performance Management (APM)
A process that uses asset condition monitoring technology to assess asset health and detect degradation so that planned interventions can occur with the goal of reducing unplanned failures
Asset Strategy Management (ASM)
A process that manages reliability strategy over time to ensure that the optimal reliability strategy is on every asset and in alignment with the performance goals of the organization at all times
Availability
The proportion of time an item or system is available to operate

Terms and Definitions

Big Data

The study of data sets that are so big and complex that traditional data processing applications are inadequate to deal with them

Cause

The reason, not the effect, of a failure; In reliability strategy development, it is critical to understand the cause of the failure mode because routine maintenance targets the cause

CMMS

An acronym for computerized maintenance management system; A system used to manage maintenance work and support a work execution management process

Consequence

The undesirable outcome of a failure as specified in a corporation's risk management framework

Corrective Action

A maintenance task that is completed as a result of an inspection or monitoring task; Example: an inspection identifies a bearing is degrading, so the corrective action would be to replace the bearing in a planned manner

Criticality

Derived from the likelihood of failure and the consequence of the failure, it is a useful measure that illustrates how much an item impacts or could impact performance and, therefore, can be used to support prioritization of the reliability strategy improvement work

Deep Learning

A subset of machine learning based on learning data representations, as opposed to task-specific algorithms

EAM	
	An acronym for enterprise asset management system
Failure	
	Occurs when an item no longer performs the required function
Failure Effect	
	The result of the failure; Similar to the consequence, but might be more descriptive or specific to the asset, whereas the consequence is aligned to the categories agreed upon in the corporate risk framework
Failure Mode	
	Describes the engineering reason for the failure
FMEA	
	An acronym for failure mode and effects analysis; A structured process to document the function, functional failures, failure modes and the effects those failure modes have
FMECA	
	An acronym for failure mode, effects and criticality analysis; Builds on a FMEA by including a likelihood so that a criticality can be calculated
Function	
	Documents a single performance requirement for an item, thus an item may have several functions
IIoT	
	An acronym for Industrial Internet of Things; A network of devices embedded with sensors that enable them to collect and connect data

Inspection

A routine task that involves checking the condition of an item with the intent of detecting any degradation associated with a failure mode

LCC

An acronym for lifecycle costing; An economic analysis that determines the total cost of ownership of an item, asset, or system for its entire lifecycle

Likelihood

The probability of an event occurring, often expressed in categories and in alignment with the corporate risk framework, such as once per year

Machine Learning

A field of computer science that uses statistical techniques to give computer systems the ability to "learn" with data

Master Data

Any content associated with assets, including asset information, materials, maintenance plans, etc., that record any information that is used to manage the assets

MTA

An acronym for maintenance task analysis; A subjective review process based solely on opinion, whereby current maintenance tasks are assessed and adjusted by subject matter experts without any analysis of failure modes or any calculation or quantification

MTBF

An acronym for mean time between failures; Calculated by adding together the times between each failure occurrence and dividing by the number of failures

MTTF

An acronym for mean time to failure; Calculated by adding the operational time between each failure (excluding off-line or repair times) and dividing by the number of failures

MTTR

An acronym for mean time to repair; Calculated by totaling the repair times and dividing by the number of repairs to get the average time to affect the repair.

Pattern Recognition

Closely related to artificial intelligence and machine learning, it is the automated recognition of patterns in data

P-F Interval

The time between detecting a potential failure and an actual functional failure; A key element for deriving appropriate inspection intervals, it can be thought of as the advanced warning time you have from when asset degradation is detected to when it will fail in service

PMO

An acronym for preventive maintenance optimization; A process of the reliability strategy review whereby you start with the current maintenance plans, rather than failure modes and attaching current tasks to them; Depending on the PMO variant applied, it is likely the process does not include appropriate evaluation of the tasks

Preventive

Tasks concerned with restoring condition in some capacity, which may include a replacement, so that future failures are prevented; Only applicable on failure modes and causes that exhibit age-related failure mechanisms

RAMS

An acronym for reliability, availability, maintainability and safety; Studies are typically completed for new projects to ensure the equipment, systems and reliability strategy deliver the required balance of risk, cost and performance

RBD

An acronym for reliability block diagram; Used to predict or forecast the performance of a system from a reliability, availability and, at times, capacity perspective; Boolean logic-based diagrams that represent system buffers, redundancies and operating practices related to system performance

RBI

An acronym for risk-based inspection; A methodology for determining task intervals based on risk, rather than a set time interval

RCM

An acronym for reliability-centered maintenance; An accepted analysis methodology or process to develop routine tasks that enable the item or asset to continue to perform the required function(s)

Reliability

The likelihood an item will operate for a desired period of time before failure

Reliability Strategy
A maintenance plan of routine tasks designed to achieve a long-term or overall aim
Risk
The potential loss caused by equipment failure; The product of severity (i.e., consequence) and likelihood
Routine Maintenance or Routine Tasks
Tasks performed on a set cadence, such as calendar time or usage rate, that make up the maintenance plan and collectively constitute the reliability strategy
Severity
The impact or consequence of a failure; Typically, a risk framework is comprised of set levels of severity, such as low, moderate, high and very high; In a risk category, such as safety or financial, each level of severity would have an example as a guideline
Tactics
Refers to routine maintenance tasks since they represent the actions that are part of the maintenance plan
Unplanned
A failure of an asset that occurs when it's not expected; Unplanned failures quite often take the asset out of operations unexpectedly and typically take more resources to repair because of consequential damage that may occurs

Weibull Analysis

The use of the Weibull distribution, a very flexible distribution effective at representing typical asset failure characteristics

Work or Task Instruction

Documents how to perform a maintenance task; Typically takes the format of required steps to follow to complete the task, complemented with pictures and/or illustrations

Work Execution Management (WEM)

A process covering the aspects of performing maintenance work, including triggering work, planning and scheduling, issuing work and gaining feedback

Introduction

Several unique challenges exist in asset intensive industries:

1. Performance is largely driven by the performance of critical assets;
2. Asset maintenance and renewal is a significant, controllable cost;
3. Asset failures can lead to the realization of significant risk.

Most organizations recognize the impact that poor reliability does and/or can have on their business outcomes and, thus, have attempted to address their reliability issues.

Predominantly, their attempts have involved placing reliability engineers or improvement engineers into the organization. These specialists very clearly have accountability for reliable asset performance. At the very least, an existing role within the organizational structure is assigned accountability for asset reliability.

Almost all organizations have invested, in some cases more than once, in the implementation of an enterprise asset management (EAM) system or a computerized maintenance management system (CMMS) to support world-class work execution management (WEM).

Predictive maintenance (PdM) technologies, as they become available, may have been tested and/or implemented to provide warning of an impending failure.

However, what has been proven over the last two decades is that simply placing reliability engineers within an organization, implementing effective work execution management and utilizing the latest predictive technologies do not solve the reliability problem.

Even in organizations considered to have world-class asset management, they still experience unplanned failures and are driven to improve performance and reduce costs. In most cases, even within these top quartile organizations, improvement is predominantly reactive, meaning an improvement occurs as the result of an analysis and investigation after an undesirable event.

Furthermore, in the absence of any supporting process and framework, pursuing a culture of reliability will deliver some benefit, but most certainly will not achieve its full potential.

The business case

Once selected, installed and commissioned, the reliability and performance that any asset delivers will be based predominantly on how it is operated and maintained.

The impact of operations will be considered outside the scope of this book, but it will look closely at the connection between performance and how assets are maintained. It is no surprise, then, that how an asset is maintained has a significant impact on the performance that will be realized. This means the reliability strategy, which is made up of the routine maintenance tasks to be performed, when they are performed (i.e., on what interval) and how they are performed, is a critical element for delivering the required performance.

It is these routine tasks, when designed correctly, deliver the desired balance of cost, risk and performance.

In most asset intensive industries, building a business case for improving reliability is somewhat of a trivial process, providing that the connection is made from reliability improvement to business outcomes.

Quite simply, an extra one percent of availability from your assets, one percent less unplanned downtime, a ten percent reduction in unplanned failure, or a five percent reduction in maintenance costs are all significant enough to justify a focus on reliability improvement.

Ask yourself:
- What does one percent of system downtime mean to your business?

- What does a ten percent increase in risk of a major incident mean to your business?
- What does a ten percent reduction in the maintenance budget represent?

The answers almost always justify a focus on reliability improvement. Furthermore, it is critical that questions like these are asked and answered so that a quantified improvement gap can be identified.

The problem

Given the opportunity and value that can be delivered by reliability, many organizations have been through a reliability strategy development or review project, sometimes more than once at the same facility. The purpose each time is to arrive at an agreed reliability strategy that is comprised of a maintenance plan with associated routine tasks to deliver the objectives of the organization.

It is here where the challenges begin. Firstly, the difficulty most organizations have in translating the recommended maintenance plans into the required master data standards for the EAM system means that, in many cases, the revised maintenance plans never actually make it into the EAM system. Countless reliability studies have been completed and yet not implemented.

Around 80% of organizations do not currently review their reliability strategy based on performance feedback.

Secondly, even if the revised maintenance plans make it into the EAM system, they are rarely, if ever, reviewed and updated. Any operating system and business climate is dynamic, in that equipment duties may change, operating context may change, business costs and/or tolerable risks may change and the level of data available about any variable associated with maintenance plan development may change. It is easy to see that if a maintenance plan stays the same while the whole system is changing, before long the maintenance plan originally developed most likely will not deliver the desired level of performance.

Thirdly, there is typically no governance and control of the reliability strategy. It is here where most organizations deviate from the ISO55000 guidelines. If a person with the correct access permission within the organization's EAM system can simply change reliability strategy related content, such as task descriptions, task intervals and which tasks are performed, with little or no requirement for review, approval, justification, or logging the reason for the change, then clearly the maintenance plan can deviate from the agreed maintenance plan. As such, performance is compromised and there is likely an unknown and undesirable level of risk.

One of the reasons for this lack of governance and control of maintenance plans on an ongoing basis is largely the perception that typical work execution management processes and an EAM system provide this functionality. In reality, of course, this is not the case.

What's missing, of course, is a dedicated process to manage the reliability strategy on an ongoing basis. Deciding what tasks to perform and the way to perform them should be connected to the current operational context and available data.

The point here is that setting a reliability strategy is not a one-off, project type activity. Rather, it is a dynamic process to ensure that the best reliability strategy is deployed to all your assets, all the time, keeping pace with the changing operational environment.

Driving culture with process and triggers

It is common for organizations to pursue a culture of reliability. A legitimate pursuit, however, is destined for failure if attempted in isolation from associated processes and triggers.

It is possible to educate people, provide knowledge and state intent. Unfortunately, people only put knowledge into practice and develop ongoing habits when there is a reason to do so. For example, we get into a car and immediately put on a seat belt. We have developed the habit of putting on the seat belt. Initially, this habit was developed through the implementation of a law that made it illegal to travel in a car without wearing a seat belt.

The knowledge that seat belts reduce the risk of injury was not, on its own, enough to establish a culture of seat belt wearers. A law had to be introduced, meaning a fine would be imposed if you were caught without wearing one. This requirement was enough to develop a culture of seat belt wearers.

The same goes for developing a culture of reliability. Intent alone is not enough; the knowledge that high reliability is good, is not enough. A requirement must be established to drive all the practices and allow the knowledge to be put into action, habits to be developed and a culture to emerge.

Asset strategy management provides that requirement. It allows a culture to develop, delivers reliability dynamically across the asset's life and will establish which organizations will be successful.

SECTION 1

A Typical Reliability Environment

We have reliability engineers, but no reliability.

In most industrial plants, the pursuit of reliability improvement has been in place in some fashion since the early to mid-1990s. The first step for most organizations was placing reliability engineers within the organizational structure.

In these early days, the term reliability was undefined in most organizations and, in many ways, this remains true. In some organizations, a reliability engineer was responsible for reliability strategy review and, in other cases, root cause analysis (RCA) or equipment condition monitoring, such as vibration and/or oil analysis.

As is often still the case, organizations talk about and even calculate what they call a reliability metric, yet it's an availability figure or, worse still, based on a unique calculation they have derived.

In almost all industrial cases, the role of a reliability engineer has the requirement to improve availability, thus probably should be called availability engineer, or perhaps better still, performance/improvement engineer.

To clear it up:

Reliability is the ability to perform a required function under given conditions for a given time.

Availability is the ability of an item to be in a state to perform a required function under given conditions at a given instant of time, or in average, over a given time interval, assuming the required external resources are available.

These two definitions represent accepted definitions from the International Organization for Standardization (ISO) and are accurate and correct. But, here is a practical adaptation to help people understand the difference:

Reliability is the likelihood an item will operate for a desired period of time before failure.

Availability is the proportion of time an item or system is available to operate.

Let's take an extreme case, assuming no other operational or process implications. Would you rather have a component that fails once a month for one minute or one that fails once a year for one month?

This is a case where the component with the poor reliability yields much greater availability and is probably the preferred option. This is, of course, provided the impacts of failure are associated with production or process downtime and are not failures that have critical event occurrences, such as an explosion, fire, or safety impacts.

Naturally, it all depends on the operations or process dependencies, but it does prove the point that you should be really clear about what you are trying to improve and what delivers the most value to the organization.

Any given site

At almost all industrial sites nowadays, some form of reliability engineer is in place. It is commonplace to call them analysis and improvement engineers, improvement engineers, or some similar play on the term. Fundamentally, however, there is a resource or team with the accountability for asset reliability and availability.

With the creation of the reliability function within organizations in the early days, it was typical, and in many cases remains true, for either smart, young engineers or experienced trades-based personnel to fill these roles. There was not, and still no, undergraduate degree in reliability engineering.

Some argue the reliability discipline warrants its own undergraduate degree, while others argue that reliability engineers can be from another engineering discipline and trained within the reliability function. This book promotes the stance that a reliability undergraduate degree is warranted, whereby reliability engineers would be specialists in all facets of data analysis, reliability techniques and analysis, problem-solving and business acumen. The reasoning is that the principles of reliability engineering are generic and applicable across all typical industrial engineering disciplines.

Certainly, in the recent past, there has been an explosion of available postgraduate certificates, diplomas and postgraduate degrees in reliability, all supporting the development of graduate engineers or experienced technicians in the concepts of reliability.

The history and evolution of filling reliability roles is important because it demonstrates the lack of training, support, education, process and technology to deliver the functional requirement. It was not uncommon, for example, to get moved from a mechanical engineering role to a reliability engineering role with nothing more than a title change and a new position description.

In fact, this was my first exposure to reliability engineering!

No wonder reliability, availability and performance didn't really improve in any sustainable way.

Of course, over the years, inroads have been made to the availability of education and support to reliability roles. However, the process and technology support that would drive improvement in a sustainable way is still absent.

What one typically finds on most industrial sites:
- A Reliability Team is in place:
  - They may be site-based, corporate-based, or both;
  - Usually a mix of young engineers and experienced, practical personnel.
- Limited reliability strategy review is occurring;
- Any reliability strategy development or review that is occurring is piecemeal and spread across spreadsheets or different applications;
- No or limited approval of any reliability strategy changes;
- The team has challenges with knowing what to work on and has limited resources to execute the work;
- There are similar assets on-site or within the organization with different reliability strategies and you don't know if that's justified or which strategy is best;
- There are localized areas of reliability excellence, but you can't leverage those across the asset base;
- The work execution management system and process allow reliability strategies and tactics to be changed with no review, or in other cases, the reliability strategy is locked down with a rigid, time-consuming management of change (MOC) process;
- You are not sure if what is being executed matches the agreed reliability strategy (if that is documented anywhere);
- Any reliability strategy review is executed as a project, not a process.

What this typically leads to is:
- No line of sight from work that is being executed in the field to the reliability analysis that justifies the task and the interval. Ultimately, this means when unplanned failures occur, there is no easy way to:
  - Extract the relevant, current maintenance plans from the EAM system;

- Trace them back to the completed reliability analysis, the failure mode being addressed, or justification of the reliability strategy, including a full audit trail of the history.
- The reliability team gets bogged down in conducting root cause analysis investigations. The team probably completes a top ten analysis and attempts to work its way through the list by conducting relevant RCAs.

What's happening fundamentally is that the organization is performance-led. In other words, it is being led by the performance it is getting. There is no looking forward, only looking backward. The top ten analysis is a rear view look at the worst stuff that's happened!

The organization is responding to the performance it is getting with no, or at best, limited, view on driving the performance it wants.

It is key to understand why this has become the typical site reliability landscape. Quite simply, there is no process that supports any other way of working.

1. How often do you review reliability strategies?
2. On what assets?
3. What's the process you follow?
4. Where's the data captured?
5. Who approves any changes?
6. Who implements the outcomes?
7. How do you know whether any changes deliver the outcomes you want?
8. When do you need to review/update it again?

So, there is no defined process for reliability strategy review and update, or, even if there is, what's always missing is any kind of trigger to start the review process.

The focus

RCA investigations, on the other hand, have a natural trigger, in that an event of significance has occurred, usually quite visible to the organization, so action must be taken.

Therefore, even when the RCA investigation process is informal, with limited support and technology, the RCA still gets done because of the trigger that starts the process.

This, of course, doesn't necessarily mean the RCA is completed well. In fact, in most cases, RCA investigations do not find a set of cause and effect relationships of significance and, therefore, do not lead to effective solutions that prevent reoccurrence of the problem.

So, RCA investigations become the focal point for reliability engineers. What's fascinating to find is that in most cases, the reliability folks will report that they have a backlog of RCAs to complete. This fact alone should indicate that the strategy of just completing RCAs is ineffective or, at the very least, the RCAs being completed are ineffective.

This lack of driving performance outcomes and allowing reliability engineers to be performance led is leading to a cycle of reaction.

The outcome

There is only one outcome to these typical environments and that is underperformance. This likely will have the associated problems of high costs and unknown risk levels. Ultimately, the organization is not in control of the asset. There is no governance of the reliability strategy decision and related content.

There are two possibilities:
1. Reliability strategy related content is being changed, informally, without overview, analysis, review and approval;
2. Reliability strategy related content is not changing at all because the MOC process is so rigid.

Both possible environments, which usually depend on the industry sector, lead to undesirable outcomes.

The reliability strategy should be changing constantly for a range of reasons, such as:

- Operational context changes;
- Changes in market conditions;
- Equipment ages;
- Technology changes;
- Fixed cost changes;
- Organizational priorities change.

Over 80% of organizations do not have a formal compliance check in place to ensure routine tasks within their EAM system are aligned to the agreed reliability strategy

In environment one in Figure 1, the reliability strategy is changed informally. It is likely not changing at all in alignment with the changing environment. This leads to an unknown, potentially undesirable level of risk.

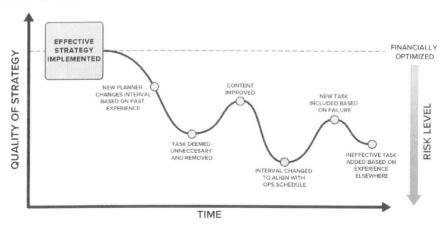

Figure 1: How risk exposure changes as reliability strategy content is updated over time

In environment two in Figure 2, the reliability strategy rarely changes, mainly because of the difficulty. It certainly does not keep alignment to the changing environment.

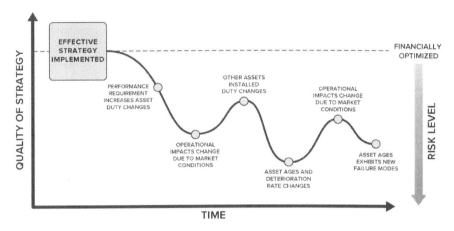

Figure 2: How risk changes over time if strategy content is fixed

So, the reliability strategy is either changing in ways it shouldn't, or not changing at all when it should.

Over 70% of organizations do not have a formal, consistent process to ensure the appropriate review of reliability strategy changes

The staggering reality is that most organizations are literally ignorant to the level of risk with which they are operating based on their existing reliability strategies. The unplanned failures still being experienced are not unforeseeable, most could and should be addressed by a reliability strategy that's dynamic and always aligned to the changing operational environment.

To illustrate this point, let's take an example scenario.

- An asset fails due to a specific failure mode, on average, once per year.

- When it fails, the asset is out of service for eight hours.
- Outages cost $1,000 per hour in lost production.
- The cost of the repair is $100 per hour for labor and $1,000 for the spare.
- The asset is currently inspected for this failure mode every week. The inspection takes fifteen minutes.
- For the sake of the math, let's say the inspection is one hundred percent accurate and any degradation detected during the inspection allows for the repair to be conducted in a planned outage where the organization won't incur the lost production costs.

In this simple environment, if the organization just lets the asset fail and repairs it, the total cost (TC) over a ten-year period is $98,000.

This is calculated by:

- 10 failures x (8 hours x $100 per hour for labor) + $1,000 spare +(8 hours x $1,000 per hour outage cost)

If recalculated with the inspection turned on, the total cost is:

TC = inspection costs + planned repair costs

> Remember that the inspection is one hundred percent effective. So, the inspection detects when the failure mode is likely to occur and plans a repair to avoid the unplanned failure.

So, TC = $31,150

This equates to about one third the cost of the run to failure scenario.

Let's assume the required analysis is done and the weekly inspection is an optimal routine task. The organization implements the reliability strategy. But, let's say no degradation is detected after six months, so it is decided (incorrectly) to extend the interval. Or, perhaps there is a change in another plan that this task can be aligned to, so the interval is extended. Or, someone comes to the organization with experience and the opinion that the interval can be extended.

There are several reasons why a reliability strategy gets changed, but the reality is the change takes place with no reliability analysis or a flawed reliability analysis.

Let's say, for example, the interval is extended to two weeks rather than one week. The TC becomes $63,600.

The inspection is no longer effective. The interval is too great for the degradation's characteristics. Some of the impeding failures are detected, but some are missed, resulting in some unplanned failures.

In practice, what is happening within plants is that people are intending to improve the performance or reduce costs, but without a sound, reliability-based review, it is very easy to make serious errors that lead to significant impacts. In the previous example, the numbers assume a fixed P-F interval (defined later in the book, but think of it as the warning or degradation time) of one week. This means inspecting at one week or less will detect the degradation and a planned repair can be completed.

If extended to two weeks, the inspections are too far apart and the degradation can happen between inspections and the failure occurs in an unplanned manner.

In reality, of course, the numbers are not so cut and dried. But what is certain, is that reliability strategies in any system have been changed, with good intent, but without due diligence. Therefore, it puts the organization at an unknown, but probably increased, level of risk of failure.

If the organization goes back to the one week inspection strategy, the TC is $31,150. To illustrate the impact of good WEM, let's say through sound work execution management principles, the efficiency of the repair activity improves.

For illustration purposes, let's say efficiency improves by twenty-five percent, meaning the duration of the repair activity takes six hours rather than eight, which could be achieved through improvements, such as reduced logistical delays associated with materials being available or ensuring the asset is ready for maintenance when the tradesperson arrives.

In this scenario, with a weekly inspection and an improvement in WEM efficiency, the TC reduces from $31,150 to $29,100.

While this is a very specific example with set parameters, the principles are universal in that reliability strategy changes will generally have a much more significant impact on performance and total costs than efficient work that is delivered by the WEM process.

SECTION 2

The Opportunity

The performance you have is a result of the asset you have and how you operate and care for it

From an asset's perspective, as shown in Figure 3, the performance you get from any given asset depends on the inherent reliability, how the asset is operated and how it is maintained.

At a simplistic level, it is based on what the asset is capable of, how it is treated and how it is looked after.

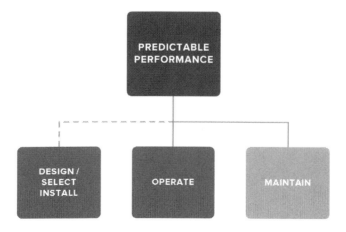

Figure 3: The drivers of performance

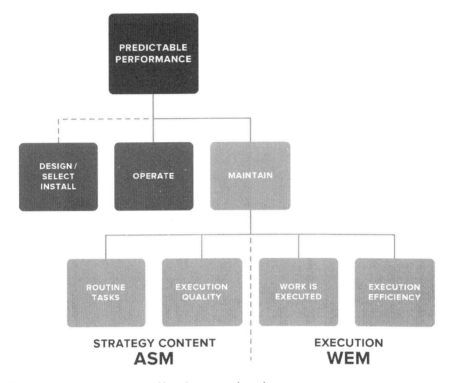

Figure 4: Maintenance effectiveness levels

This book, of course, is concerned with how organizations look after assets and, specifically, the performance impact that asset care (i.e., routine tasks) can have.

As shown in Figure 4, the maintenance related performance is predominantly based on four simple elements:

1. What the organization chooses to do;
2. How it chooses to do it;
3. Doing it;
4. Doing it efficiently.

What an organization chooses to do and how it chooses to do it are elements of the reliability strategy for the asset.

Doing the work and doing it efficiently is the execution of the reliability strategy.

Elements of reliability strategy related content are:
> **Routine Tasks:** Which tasks to complete at which interval and by whom;
>
> **Execution Quality:** The quality of the work completed, which is delivered by succinct, practical work instructions that describe how to correctly perform tasks.

Key elements of the work execution management process are:
> **Work Is Executed:** Ensuring tasks that constitute the reliability strategy are executed and completed;
>
> **Execution Efficiency:** Planning, scheduling and sound logistics so that all execution work is complete as efficiently as possible with minimal delays and/or downtime.

It is important to note here that while execution quality is being driven by concise, succinct and complete work instructions, which are instructions on how to complete tasks, there is also a dependency on the technical competency of those completing the work. This book does not cover the area of technical competency, other than to note that during any reliability strategy setting and routine task development, the current competency and maturity of the organization must be considered.

While work execution management as a concept is somewhat mature, in almost all asset management systems, there is no process to manage the reliability strategy and related quality content on an ongoing basis. Typically, reliability strategy related decisions are made as part of an initial installation project, EAM system implementation, or a one-off reliability strategy review project. In other words, reliability strategy is commonly **set**, but not **managed**.

Over 80% of organizations do not have a formal review process for reliability strategies beyond addressing major failures

SECTION 2

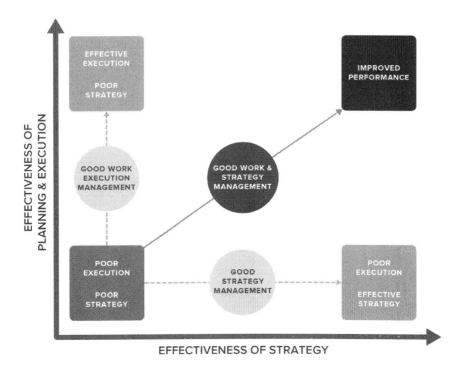

Figure 5: WEM versus ASM

Figure 5 illustrates how even with world-class work execution management in place, if you are executing the wrong reliability strategy, then performance will be less than ideal.

An extreme example of this can be a typical car service. The efficiency and speed at which a mechanic can perform a service demonstrates the effectiveness of the work execution management process. This would manifest in the mechanic being available when the car arrives, all required tools and materials being available to the mechanic and the car being cleaned and ready to maintain.

However, if the only routine task the mechanic performs during the service is to ensure the radio is tuned to the local stations, then the reliability strategy is very poor and contains an ineffective routine task(s). Future performance will not be influenced and the company will default to a performance-led environment whereby mechanics will react to future failures of the car.

Alternatively, the reliability strategy is very sound, so routine tasks have been generated using reliability principles and are aligned to performance objectives. However, the execution is very inefficient, meaning the car is waiting for the mechanic to arrive, the mechanic then waits for parts and equipment to arrive and the whole execution is much longer than it should be.

In this scenario, the outcome is still less than ideal, although it is likely overall performance will be better since less failures typically have a greater impact than shorter outages.

As noted previously, an important aspect is that reliability strategies need constant review to remain aligned to performance objectives and the operational environment. Thus, reliability strategies need to be **managed**. This requires the implementation of an ongoing asset strategy management (ASM) process that must become part of the asset management function's business as usual (BAU) operations.

Naturally, organizations should pursue both WEM and ASM processes. The key point to remember is that ASM is a separate process requiring resources and technology, but it will likely deliver much greater value than the WEM process.

SECTION 3

Work Execution Management (WEM)

Work execution management delivers efficiency, not reliability

There is a widely held concept that you cannot add reliability to an asset through maintenance. While this is true, it is not necessarily reliability that organizations are interested in improving. It is the availability of the asset and reducing any impact from maintenance interventions by not having failures occur in an unplanned fashion.

With that in mind, maintenance can certainly improve performance by applying the right reliability strategy.

However, the concept has taken hold and it is almost certainly misinterpreted to some degree. This is likely because one thing is for certain: WEM without reliability strategy does not deliver any significant improvement.

Using a car example again, if no maintenance is performed over the life of the car, it will fail more and be off the road longer than the same car properly maintained. The unmaintained car also has a higher risk of failing in an unplanned manner that may cause catastrophic consequences.

Implementing sound work execution management practices when the unmaintained car fails may get it back on the road again slightly quicker than without sound WEM in place, but it likely will be a marginal performance improvement.

So, that brings us back to the same fundamental concept that WEM is about ensuring that you execute what you agree to execute and that you can execute the activity efficiently.

What is WEM?

Work execution management is essentially the process of managing work. The objective is to support the most efficient execution of work.

The key elements of WEM is a well-defined work management process and an appropriate technical solution that can support the process.

Several well-known enterprise resource planning (ERP) systems contain an EAM system and there are many stand-alone EAM systems. These technical solutions are mature and offer a range of plug-ins, add-ons and base product functionality that support efficient execution in all industry verticals.

The WEM process is usually constructed using standard business process mapping techniques, at times with swim lanes that notate the accountable resource for each step.

Essentially, the process shows the flow of work from the initial trigger that work needs to be done to approval to do the work, planning, scheduling, execution and feedback on completion.

The technical solution supports the process with the required functionality and a matched workflow. In an environment with sound work execution management practices, when technicians are handed a job, they are handed a work pack with all the relevant details of the job and detailed instructions on how to execute the work. When they arrive at the job site, the asset is ready to be maintained, perhaps turned off and cleaned, and any special equipment and the required materials are already at the job site. This environment delivers an efficient execution of the work and minimizes unproductive time of the asset.

WEM continues to evolve, mainly by using available technology to support digitization, where relevant, of the process. Job details and instruction content can be delivered and interacted with on a mobile device and task instruction content can be delivered via instructional videos or even through smart glasses.

What does WEM deliver?

Exclude for a moment any changes to the reliability strategy you have in place. As such, any fundamental improvement in WEM will reduce the unproductive time of assets by shortening the time required for repair. WEM is an efficiency game!

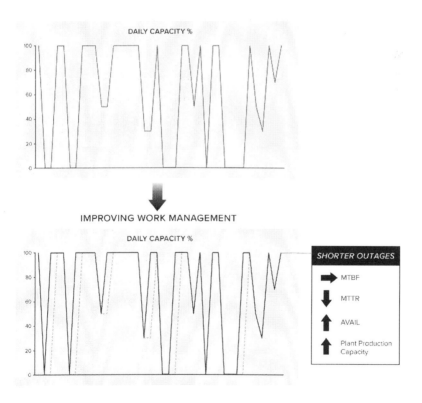

Figure 6: The effect of sound WEM practices

As Figure 6 shows, the improvement in performance through a sound WEM is minor because you still have the same number of outages; they are just shorter.

The reliability strategy, however, can influence the number of failures or outages you see.

Limitations of WEM

Efficiently executing the wrong reliability strategy is, at best, wasting resources

Work execution management is a process designed, quite simply, to manage work. It literally focuses on efficient and effective execution of the work required to be done. Determining the reliability strategy and the tasks that should be executed to deliver the performance you want is outside of the WEM process and simply provides one of the triggers for the WEM process to begin. Typically, the WEM triggers are either system generated work, which is work to do at some regular interval, or emergent work, which is work that becomes apparent, perhaps via a routine inspection.

Because the technical solution utilized to support the WEM process is commonly set up with role-based permission access, there is a perception of some level of control of the reliability strategy related content. Further, because there is a defined WEM process with measurable key performance indicators (KPIs), there is a perception of some level of governance. This control and governance are based around the WEM process, not the maintenance plans. Therefore, in the absence of any defined process to manage the maintenance plans, there is no governance and control around them. This has a significant bearing on the risk carried and the performance realized.

The key here is that the WEM process ensures an efficient execution of the reliability strategy. However, the reliability strategy should be managed over time through ASM. The connection point between the two processes is the reliability strategy related content, but ASM is the master system or system of record for that content.

So, setting reliability strategy is key to delivering high performance!

SECTION 4

Setting a Reliability Strategy

Reliability Strategy: The actions you are going to take to deliver the performance you want

Definition

What is a reliability strategy?

Figure 7: The elements of a reliability strategy

It consists of three key elements:

1. Routine maintenance and corrective action plans;
2. Asset and/or fleet level decisions;
3. Portfolio level decisions.

Routine maintenance and corrective action plans

The routine maintenance and corrective action plans document the activities that are going to be executed on a daily, weekly, monthly and yearly basis or at some kind of usage type interval, for example, an inspection type task that results in necessary corrective action because the asset is in a state of deterioration. Basically, you are documenting what regular activities are going to be completed on some frequency, by whom, what materials and equipment they need, any support required, the required operational status of the equipment, etc. Also documented are the resources required for any corrective actions that are essential across the life of the asset, who completes them, what materials and equipment are needed, other support required, etc.

Where required, any detailed work instruction content, which describes how to complete the task, should be included as part of this routine maintenance and corrective actions content.

Like all reliability strategy related content, these work instructions will need refinement, updates and review over time to match the changing component, technology and environment.

All this content is what constitutes the master data that will make up the maintenance plans in the EAM system.

Asset and/or fleet level decisions

Asset or fleet level decisions are beyond the routine maintenance and corrective actions plans and constitute the overall reliability strategy for the asset or fleet. This reliability strategy related content could be major asset optimum replacement age, repair/replace decision points, or number of assets required within the system or fleet to deliver the operational target.

Naturally, there is a connection between the routine maintenance and corrective action plans and the asset level reliability strategies. In fact, all the data, knowledge and experience used to generate the routine maintenance and corrective actions will form the basis of the data required for the asset level strategy decision.

In many organizations, this level of reliability strategy decision is not completed at all or, perhaps, only at the project stage for new assets.

There is the potential for enormous value to be realized through the expansion or contraction of assets within a system based on new technology, greater individual asset availability, or changing market conditions.

It is also an important step in establishing whether system targets can be met. There have been many projects where, upon analysis, the current fleet or system literally cannot achieve the desired system availability or capacity, even if world-class performance for every asset was achieved.

Portfolio level decisions

Portfolio decisions are value-based investment optimization decisions, considering all potential or requested investments. It is more easily illustrated with an example:

Let's say, you have some major pumps that are part of a critical pumping system. You can develop the routine maintenance and corrective action plans and you can determine how many pumps are required in the system and at what age they should be replaced. If you determine that the pumps require replacement next year at a cost of twenty million dollars, that is an investment you will request of the business to support operations.

A portfolio is made up of all the required investments, which could be asset related plus others, that are managed under the same constraints. The most common constraint, of course, is financial.

If all the required investments total one hundred million dollars to be spent next year, but the organization only has sixty million dollars in capital to invest, then an optimization needs to be completed.

A portfolio optimization should be completed for investments that have been valued using a consistent value framework so all are valued using the same scale. The investments data also should be time related. In other words, what is the value over time that the investment delivers and what are the risks or losses that are mitigated by the investment?

The optimization process will then consider moving investments on the time scale and consider different alternatives and combinations of investments to determine the best investments to complete that will deliver the most value to the organization within the financial constraints in place.

The whole point of connecting right from the routine maintenance and corrective plans, through asset level decisions, to portfolio decisions is to cater to a feedback loop. For example, the pump replacement was determined optimal to complete next year when considered in isolation. However, its replacement is deferred when completing the optimization because other investments deliver greater value. So, the routine maintenance and corrective action plans likely need to be altered to support the required life extension of the pumps.

Value

Enormous value can be obtained by getting the reliability strategy right. This can be done by using three main avenues:

1. Reducing the number of unplanned outages, therefore improving performance of the asset, assets, or system;
2. Reducing costs through a reduced corrective maintenance effort and not overspending on routine maintenance;
3. Reducing the risk of low probability, high consequence events.

As shown in Figure 8, the improvement in performance through sound reliability strategy can be significant because the number of failures is reduced, leading to significant increases in performance and reduction in costs.

Setting a Reliability Strategy

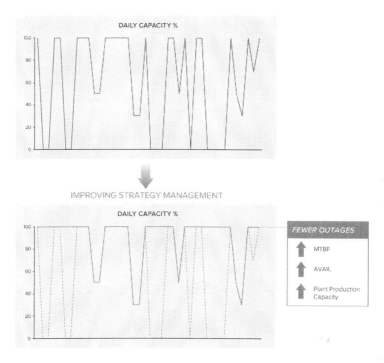

Figure 8: The effectiveness of sound reliability strategy

Methodologies

For the three elements of reliability strategy, there are some key methodologies that have proven to yield the best outcomes:

1. Routine maintenance and corrective action task development is best completed using some key concepts of reliability-centered maintenance (RCM) or one of its many derivatives. The key concepts are defined in some detail in upcoming sections.
2. Asset and fleet level decisions are best made using reliability block diagrams (RBDs) and lifecycle costing (LCC) analysis.
3. Portfolio optimization is best completed using a value-based asset investment planning (AIP), management and optimization analysis.

By far, the most crowded technical space in reliability strategy is in developing or optimizing routine maintenance tasks and corrective actions. This is largely because there has been a proliferation of RCM variants developed by competing software and services companies.

The upcoming sections and much of the ASM content presented in this book focus on setting, reviewing and conducting ongoing management of routine maintenance strategies because, quite simply, it is this area where most organizations can make the easiest and best gains.

RCM and variants

Reliability-centered maintenance, with origins in the aviation industry, entered general industry on the back of RCM II, authored by John Moubray and first published in 1992, with a second edition in 1997. Since then, there have been several different variants of RCM in the marketplace by competing organizations that provide software and/or consulting services. Typically, the underlying principles of the RCM process remain consistent, with the key elements being:

1. The RCM process is about preserving equipment function.
2. Failure modes are developed that can cause the loss of function. This is also known as functional failure.
3. Failure effects are documented. At times, this is specified as failure effect and then impact of failure or a single consequence of failure. Usually, the quantification of impact of failure aligns to any existing risk management framework or severity rating guide.
4. The likelihood of failure is specified. Depending on the variant, this is usually a simple probability, mean time between failures (MTBF), a Weibull distribution, or a semiquantitative value.
5. Routine tasks are evaluated or, alternatively, a process is followed to determine the best routine task for consideration.

There are several slightly different steps for the different variants of the RCM process, but, fundamentally, they include:

1. Identifying required function;
2. Identifying failure modes;

3. Quantifying effect and cost of failure;
4. Quantifying how often the failure occurs;
5. A form of task selection, evaluation, or optimization.

When applying some form of RCM derivative, it is important that it is based on data-driven evaluation and optimization. This means it is key to quantify all values so that a numerical based evaluation can occur.

In the earliest applications of RCM, the process, when applied practically, involved using a facilitation process for a cross-functional analysis. This ensured the function, effects, likelihoods and task information was based on the collective knowledge of the organization.

Most would agree this leads to the best outcome in terms of the quality of the content and analysis, and the ownership participants have of the results. Anyone involved in these original, fully facilitated RCM studies would agree that the output was generally top quality. They probably also would agree that the process was arduous and required a large investment in resources and time to complete.

Perhaps the worst part about these original RCM studies was the difficulty in implementing the outputs. The translation from the RCM study outputs to the EAM master data was manual and generally an afterthought of the project, rather than an identified step of the project.

Tragically, many of these early RCM studies were not implemented and contributed to the rise of the term, shelfware, meaning the outputs, usually stored in several ring binders, were literally placed in a bookshelf and never used.

Unfortunately, the time and effort to complete these early RCM studies also gave rise to the resource consuming monster description of the RCM acronym.

The third challenge practitioners saw with early RCM projects was the difficulty in utilizing existing or current maintenance plans as a starting point. While the RCM rigor cannot be denied, beginning from a blank page, rather than starting with existing maintenance tasks, seemed counterintuitive to many experienced practical participants.

The outcome of these early RCM studies, therefore, gave rise to many different variants of RCM, each attempting to address those initial challenges:

1. The significant resource requirements;
2. The difficulty in implementation;
3. The inability to utilize existing maintenance tasks or templates.

Preventive maintenance optimization (PMO)

One of the most common variants of RCM that uses an unrelated name is preventive maintenance optimization or PMO.

The basic premise of PMO is that you start with your current maintenance tasks and assign them to failure modes. This process identifies where there are several existing tasks addressing a single failure mode. For example, a component could have an operator check, electrical check and mechanical check all associated with a single failure mode.

The main opportunity, then, is to optimize the plan by consolidating current tasks, removing duplicates and improving tasks as required.

The early adoption of PMO attracted some criticism from RCM purists who claimed the process does not consider failure modes that may well exist, but are not covered by current maintenance tasks. Since the process starts with current tasks, this is, of course, a fair comment.

Several PMO processes, however, do include a step to consider other failure modes of the component not covered by current maintenance tasks.

By the same token, several RCM variants started to utilize existing plans in their processes to speed up the analysis.

In the end, the many and varied RCM and PMO processes are eerily similar and, in many cases, it comes down to product and services marketing.

What's critical is that any RCM or PMO process used or, in a general sense, any maintenance plan development or maintenance plan review and optimization process, must contain several key elements, as outlined in the next section. What the process is called is less important!

Maintenance task analysis (MTA)

Maintenance task analysis (MTA) is employed by organizations to conduct some level of maintenance plan review.

Like a PMO exercise, MTAs start with the current tasks, but rather than connecting tasks to failure modes, subject matter experts (SMEs) simply review the list of tasks for an asset or the maintenance plan and, based on their experience, challenge the effectiveness of each task.

This can be an appealing process when the organization believes it doesn't have the data to complete anything more than a subjective, expert-driven review.

The problem, of course, is a lack of real structure to these reviews and they are completely subjective. If there is more than one SME in the group, completing the review and getting them to agree is a task in itself!

The ineffectiveness of these reviews becomes starkly apparent when they are completed by SMEs one-on-one or remotely and there are more than one SME involved. There have been instances where SMEs violently disagree on single task details, such as the interval of specific tasks, when the review sheet has been sent to both SMEs for review. The individual responses show exactly how far apart SMEs can be.

So, why is it that SMEs – people considered experts in their field and knowledgeable on the assets in question – can have entirely different views? Quite simply, their views are driven by their experience and background with the assets in question and the organizations and operations where they have worked.

This lack of structure and analysis means there is no real platform to discuss the merits of the tasks and task details, so it is purely opinion that forms the basis of the decisions. In such cases, it can mean that the squeaky wheel gets the oil.

For this reason, it is rare for any kind of opinion-based review, such as MTA, to be successful in delivering changes in performance.

So which methodology works?

When it comes to setting, reviewing, or optimizing reliability strategy, what's important is making sure that the key elements required for sound reliability strategy decision-making are included in the process. What it's called has no bearing on the success of the analysis.

Section 5 covers the key elements of reliability strategy decision-making and outlines the biggest traps to ineffective decision-making.

SECTION 5
Setting a Reliability Strategy – Fundamental Concepts

It doesn't matter what you call it, but to be effective, your reliability strategy review process must be built around some key concepts

Having reviewed countless approaches to routine tasks reliability strategy review and optimization and from being involved in many more review or optimization projects, it has become apparent that there are several key concepts required to ensure a successful review or optimization project.

These following concepts assume a basic understanding of failure mode, effects and criticality analysis (FMECA), which underpins almost all reliability strategy review processes.

With a FMECA based approach, the review and optimization key concepts are:
1. Ensuring a functional based approach;
2. Ensuring tasks are connected to a failure mode;
3. Representing the characteristics of failure;
4. Quantifying the effects of failure;
5. Understanding the two fundamental task options and key aspects of each;
6. Quantitative evaluation.

Functional based

One of the enlightening moments for most students learning about RCM is the concept of maintaining to preserve equipment function, rather than maintaining the asset to some other standard, which, in practice, is usually either end of the spectrum, from maintaining to an as new condition to maintaining to ensure the asset works as designed.

Those two options may sound quite similar, but, in practice, this ranges from maintaining an asset so it looks, sounds and operates like it did when brand new to maintaining an asset that might be noisy, dirty, leaking, vibrating, inefficient, or unsafe, but still working.

The first key concept of ensuring the reliability strategy is functional based is about making sure that the plans put in place deliver the functional requirements for the asset.

The most obvious example to demonstrate the power in this concept is automobiles. Several customers can buy the same model automobile, but utilize them for entirely different purposes. For instance, the same type of vehicle could be used for:

1. Taxi service;
2. Daily city commute to work;
3. Daily highway commute to work;
4. Family car in urban setting;
5. Family car in a rural setting with unmade roads.

It is easy to see that some of these different functional requirements may require different maintenance regimes. Hence, the benefit of first identifying what the functional requirement is so the correct routine maintenance can be designed.

Another simple example is industrial pumps, which can pump all manner of product, from water to toxic to harmful chemicals. Again, it is easy to see that a harmful chemical pump would be required to contain the product, and that there is a need to maintain the asset to ensure the integrity of the containment. On the other hand, a water pump, while general containment of the water is probably desired, it might not attract quite the same level of functional requirement and, therefore, not such rigid maintenance.

It is important to note that the level at which the functional analysis is performed is critical for it to be meaningful. For a large pumping system, for example, it is usually easy to define the functional requirements of the pumping system. It involves identifying operationally why the pumping system has been installed. What is the operational reason for the pumping system? What does it need to do for the operations?

The operational reason(s) why the pumping system is there is commonly referred to as the primary function(s). Every asset then has one or more secondary functions. These can be viewed as: since the asset is there, what else does it need to do? Some examples would be containment, aesthetic and safety type functions.

Again, for the pumping system, it is quite simple to generate the required primary and secondary functions because, as an operational system, it is there to satisfy some operational requirement.

However, let's see what happens when the pumping system is broken down to its component parts of the:

1. Motor;
2. Coupling;
3. Gearbox;
4. Pump.

At this component level, the functional concept begins to fall apart and the functional requirements become a little more obscure and less meaningful. What is the function of an electric motor? Typically, the answer is to drive the coupling, gearbox and pump at a certain rpm, or something similar. At this point, the connection to the actual operational function of the asset or system is lost and the statement barely adds value.

Does this relate in a lost opportunity to ensure you are maintaining to support operational function? With an experienced practitioner, the value still can be realized through the application of the correct effects of failure. This is because the real qualitative tie-in to the operational function requirement is the effects of failure, which will be covered later in this section.

What is lost in this scenario of functional statements for components as compared to assets is the ability to identify areas where the asset cannot deliver the functional objective. This most likely occurs in mature sites where operational requirements have changed over time, but the assets have not.

So, your question may be: Why not just complete the functional analysis at the asset or system level, rather than the component level? The answer is an important one that relates to providing a successful and efficient implementation path.

If the functional analysis is completed at the asset level, then the component becomes an important aspect that is usually documented within the failure mode level detail.

In other words, if the functional analysis is completed at the pumping system level and a breakdown to the component level is missing, then the component part must be referenced somewhere and, hence, ends up in the failure mode statement. An example of this statement might be: "Motor bearing seized due to lack of lubrication."

If the component part is included in some way with the failure mode description, it can become very difficult to identify which component a connected task is on when it is implemented into a package of work in the EAM system.

What can happen is that once the resulting tasks are packaged and attached to the asset, the task descriptions are not prescriptive enough to communicate the component within the asset for which the task relates.

For example, let's say the resulting task of the previously mentioned failure mode statement is to: "Lubricate the bearing." When this gets implemented into a package of work, it will show up as a task on the pumping system. It is not clear, then, as to *which* bearing the task applies.

This subsequently leads to including the component part within the task description, for example, "Lubricate the motor outboard bearing." While this would work in theory, it also provides extra challenges. The ordering or sequencing of tasks when the component part is within the task description is a more manual exercise. Worse still, this removes the opportunity to utilize standard task descriptions and phrases.

The main benefit in the functional analysis is twofold:
1. Support the identification of the area where the assets selected or installed cannot deliver the function requirements of the operations;
2. Support the design of maintenance tasks that preserve the required function, rather than just maintain the asset.

There are two aspects to focus on to ensure both effective and efficient analysis:
1. Document the functional requirements at a level in the asset hierarchy that makes sense from an operational requirements perspective;
2. Ensure the actual component to be worked on is not housed within a failure mode and/or task description.

These focus areas support the main benefit from the functional analysis, but also ensure that templates and generic phrases can be readily utilized to speed up the effort.

Failure mode to task connection

When designing a sound reliability strategy, a good rule of thumb is to ensure that single mechanisms of failure are contained in each failure mode, rather than grouping them. Ignore the temptation to group failure mechanisms into a single failure mode statement, such as, "Failed due to wear, damage, foreign material ingress, or poor installation." While this might appear as a time saver, it leads to ineffective task design. Each of those mechanisms of failure would potentially require very different tasks at different intervals, completed by different resources.

A good definition of failure mode is that it is the engineering reason of failure. Therefore, each one should be a single reason.

Some general rules to keep in mind:

1. Try to avoid terms related to failure or failed in the statement since this forces the actual outcome to be considered. For example, "Bearing collapsed due to misalignment."
2. Assign only one routine task per failure mode. There may be some special cases where a single failure mode with the right characteristics of failure and failure effects will be optimized with more than one task, however, this should be the exception, not the rule.

The reason why it is critical for each failure mode to be one mechanism of failure is because the characteristics of failure (covered in the next section) need to be identified for each individual failure mechanism so that a true understanding of age-related failure modes and random failure modes can occur.

With this philosophy in mind, several tasks can be created on the same component, but spread across the different failure modes of the component. At times, this structure can create long task instruction documents, but they can be reduced significantly by allowing tasks to be grouped. So, it's okay to have a task description that addresses more than one failure mode and duplicates that task across all relevant failure modes. Then, when packaging into the task instruction documents, you can remove the duplicates and consolidate the number of tasks to a reasonable level.

As an example, you may have a task description that states, "Check the bearing for heat, noise and vibration." This may be a relevant task for more than one failure mode. The task is placed across the relevant failure modes, so it appears two or three times in the analysis. At the implementation stage, duplicates are removed and a single task is left.

So, the keys elements for a good failure mode and task relationship are:

1. Failure mode statements don't contain the component, but may contain the part;
2. Each failure mode is only a single failure mechanism;
3. In general, one failure mode has one routine task;
4. Task descriptions may cover a few tasks, so they can be duplicated across more than one failure mode.

The three characteristics of failure

Understanding how to represent the characteristics of failure are key to supporting:

1. Correct task selection;
2. Quantitative evaluation of task effectiveness.

The characteristics of failure describe the type of failure or, more technically, the probability of failure over time. It is critical for a sound reliability strategy review and evaluation to be able to understand and describe what the likelihood of failure is over the life of the asset. In typical cases, the timescale used is calendar time. So, for example, you might represent the likelihood of getting a car tire puncture over the life of the tire. Let's consider for a moment that punctures are typically created by driving over a sharp object. The likelihood of that happening is random. In other words, you are no more likely to drive over a sharp object next week, next month, or next year, than you are today. In this case, the likelihood of failure is constant over time.

In other cases, the likelihood of failure increases over time. In other words, an asset is more likely to fail the older it gets or the more time it is operating because it wears or degrades. Sticking with the example of the car tire, while a puncture may exhibit random behavior, the failure mechanism of tire tread wear clearly is more and more likely the further you drive and the more uses the tire sees.

SECTION 5

The simple example of the car tire illustrates some very key points:

1. The characteristics of failure should be considered for a failure mode, not the whole asset. The car tire puncture has different characteristics of failure to the worn tread.
2. Identifying the characteristics at the failure mode level is critical for appropriate routine task selection. Designing the tasks when considering a tire is difficult, whereas designing tasks for punctures and worn tread is much more structured and intuitive.

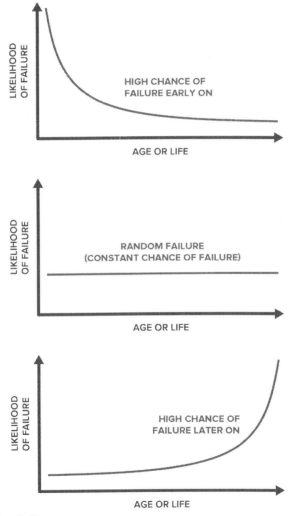

Figure 9: Key failure curves

The three main failure characteristics, as shown in Figure 9, are sometimes referred to as failure curves. They are commonly known as:

1. Infant mortality, meaning the asset is more likely to fail early in its life;
2. Random failure, meaning the asset has a constant likelihood of failure that does not change over time; this means the likelihood of failure is not related to the age of the component;
3. Wear out, meaning the likelihood of failure increases over time, age, or usage.

When put together, the three curves form what's commonly called the bathtub curve. This combined curve is typically used to describe the likelihood of failure of an entire asset or assembly. At first, there are early life failures, then useful life with a lower, seemingly random, likelihood of failure and finally an increase in the likelihood of failure as the asset or system reaches its end of life.

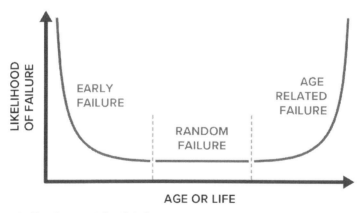

Figure 10: Equipment bathtub curve

Most people are familiar with the equipment bathtub curve displayed in Figure 10 and, in some cases, the individual elements of infant mortality, random and wear out curves. However, what's sometimes misunderstood is that these curves are representations made by the Weibull distribution. The Weibull distribution is just one of many mathematical distributions, but it is one that is effective at representing the different characteristics of equipment failure probability.

It can sound complicated, but the underlying principle is quite simple. A distribution is a line that describes a range of likely values. Typically, you have some data that you can plot on a chart, say, for example, a few equipment failures. A distribution uses the data you have to generate a representation of what you think the behavior of the full population of assets looks like.

So, let's say you had some car tire punctures in the past. Those data points can be used to determine the likelihood of experiencing a puncture over time. The job of the distribution is to fit the data points to the curve that best fits the points. In this case, the Weibull distribution is used and one of the three shapes will become apparent.

Using the Weibull distribution to represent equipment failure characteristics is commonplace because:

1. It represents all three characteristics well;
2. It has proven effective with small numbers of data points;
3. Once taught, it is easy to understand the parameters and describe either behavior experienced or a behavior one would expect in terms of the Weibull parameters.

It should be noted that several other mathematical distributions can be used to represent equipment failure and, in some cases, specific characteristics, more accurately than the Weibull distribution. This book focuses on the Weibull distribution for all the reasons previously stated and its widespread use when describing equipment failure.

It's important to remember that any given asset or failure mode of an asset can exhibit one, two, or all three of the failure characteristics or zones. Indeed, RCM uses six failure patterns, which are nothing more than one, two, or all three of the zones combined.

It is unclear exactly why only six combinations were selected for the six patterns of RCM because they don't represent the full possibility of combinations. From a practical sense, there are only a few common options when considering the characteristics of failure at a failure mode level.

In most cases, typical industrial plants do not have lots of quality failure data, meaning the analysis is occurring with a limited number of data points. In these cases, it is unlikely that a multi-zone Weibull will be the result. This means the data will only yield a single zone of the Weibull curve.

In practice, there are generally two results:

1. Random activity;
2. Age related behavior.

While data analysis can yield indications of infant mortality or early life failures, it tends to be because of inaccurate data, rather than a consistent exhibition of early life failure.

Random activity

Random activity confuses some new reliability engineers because it seems counterintuitive to have an average life for a component whose failure likelihood is random. The best way to think about and rationalize random failure is to consider accidental damage. It is an entirely random activity when your parked car gets damaged, perhaps by the car in the next space opening a car door into it or through contact with a shopping cart.

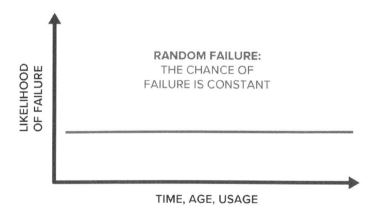

Figure 11: Random failure likelihood

So, the likelihood of that occurring is random, as represented in Figure 11. However, you can calculate the average time between damage. If you had three incidents in the last three years, then the average frequency is one per year. Hence, random activity, but, on average, occurs once per year.w

Quite often, actual data can indicate a random failure behavior even when you suspect it to be age or use related. In these instances, it is wise to dig a little deeper into the data and investigate if it is, indeed, random behavior.

Behavior will appear random when there are several causes of failure. For example, if you worked out the likelihood of failure for your car, it would appear entirely random. This is because there are so many possible failure mechanisms that there is no specific characteristics of failure apparent and everything blends into an apparent random behavior.

So, mixed failure modes can lead to a false apparent random behavior. The other main reason is that other variables are changing. For example, there are changes to the feed rate to the process, the daily duty rate, or operational time, yet you are using calendar time to calculate the characteristics of failure rather than product amount or operating hours. As such, the result will appear to be random behavior, where in fact, there is a well-defined, usage-based characteristic of failure.

Age related behavior

Age related behavior is the other key characteristic of failure. This characteristic matches intuitive expectations of most general mechanical equipment. They are installed, will operate for some expected useful life and then their likelihood of failure starts to increase, as shown in Figure 12, as the component comes to the end of its useful life and fails.

Setting a Reliability Strategy – Fundamental Concepts

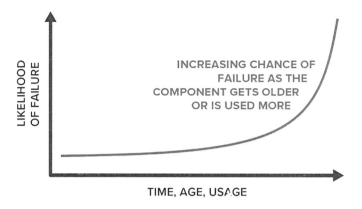

Figure 12: Age related failure likelihood (wear out)

Any item that wears through its normal use is a practical example of an age related failure characteristic, such as tire tread, chute liners, scrapers, conveyor belting, power poles, pump liners, etc.

Impacts of failure

If you can't quantify what the impact of failure is, how can you decide how much to spend to prevent it?

Understanding the effects or impact of failure is critical for the correct determination of a reliability strategy. If a functional analysis has been completed, this step becomes much easier and can be a simple selection from a pick list. For example, if the functional requirement is to deliver a certain amount of product, the functional failure may be no product. The effect of any failure mode that leads to that functional failure can be documented as the business impact associated with no product delivery.

The goal for assigning the impacts of failure is to create a pick list that is aligned to any existing corporate risk management framework. Here you will find the categories of risk the organization has identified, such as safety, environmental, production, financial, reputation, etc.

For each category of risk, the framework typically identifies the level of risk for a range of severity levels and likelihoods. The categories and severity levels can be used as the basis for the impacts of failure selection, noting that the likelihood of occurrence will come from the likelihood of failure of the associated failure mode. A typical risk matrix is presented in Figure 13.

CONSEQUENCE

FREQUENCY	VERY LOW	MINOR	MODERATE	MAJOR	CATASTROPHIC
ALMOST CERTAIN	SIGNIFICANT	SIGNIFICANT	HIGH	HIGH	HIGH
LIKELY	MEDIUM	SIGNIFICANT	SIGNIFICANT	HIGH	HIGH
MODERATE	LOW	MEDIUM	SIGNIFICANT	HIGH	HIGH
UNLIKELY	LOW	LOW	MEDIUM	SIGNIFICANT	HIGH
RARE	LOW	LOW	MEDIUM	SIGNIFICANT	HIGH

Figure 13: Risk management matrix example

What's critical is the impact of failure quantifies the impact based on the functional requirement, not just the equipment's operational state. Again, if the functional analysis has been completed, this step is rather straightforward. If the functional analysis has not been completed or not completed well, it is critical when assigning the impact of failure for the true impact on the required function of the asset to be considered and assigned.

When assigning the category of impact (e.g., safety, environment, financial) and then the severity level (e.g., very high, high, moderate, low), they should be quantified values, which may be severity level units or currency. Ideally, all categories of risk are normalized to a single scale, preferably currency, however, sometimes this is not possible. In these cases, it is okay to proceed with the analysis and when the evaluation and optimization occurs, a task can be evaluated based on risk and/or financial criteria.

Maintenance task options

The creation of several unique terms to describe different types of maintenance within different industries or organizations has generated confusion about how fundamentally simple reliability strategy development and review is. Terms commonly heard are scheduled replacement, scheduled discard, overhaul, shutdown, inspection, condition-based maintenance, corrective maintenance, condition monitoring, calibration, preventive maintenance, predictive maintenance, proactive maintenance, operator tasks, daily checks and walk-arounds, just to name a few!

It's no wonder, then, that reliability strategy development and review feels complex. But, the reality is there are only two fundamental task options from which to choose. Each reliability strategy-based routine task fits into one of two categories:

1. Preventive;
2. Predictive.

They are the only two choices. The only other alternatives are running the asset to failure or redesigning it.

If you run it to failure, you then need to plan for repairs. If the predictive maintenance strategy detects an impending failure, you need to conduct a corrective activity.

So, while this book is not concerned with changing colloquial terminology, it is important to understand the fundamental task types so they can be related to your language.

In terms of maintenance tasks, there are:

1. Failure repair tasks;
2. Preventive tasks;
3. Predictive tasks;
4. Secondary or corrective action tasks.

That's it! From a reliability strategy setting perspective, you have to decide what needs to be done and whether you are going to implement a preventive task or a predictive task.

SECTION 5

Preventive tasks

Preventive tasks are tasks where you are doing something that changes the condition in some way to prevent failure from occurring. This covers tasks like:

1. Lubrication;
2. Calibration;
3. Replacement;
4. Restoration;
5. Adjustment;
6. Cleaning, if an accumulation of dirt or debris can lead to failure.

The whole concept of preventive tasks is that if you complete the task, then failure is prevented and you won't experience the failure.

Preventive tasks are only applicable if you have age related failure characteristics. This means the likelihood of failure increases the older the asset gets or the more it is used. The goal is to complete the preventive task before the likelihood of failure increases and, thus, reset the likelihood of failure curve and prevent the failure.

Replacement is a typical example of a preventive task. For example, you replace the engine oil in your car at a specified interval. You don't check the quality of the oil, you simply choose to replace the oil at a fixed interval. You know that oil has a useful life and this act of replacement should prevent any engine failure caused by oil degradation or contamination. Note in this example the focus is on degradation of oil quality, not engine oil level.

Naturally, preventive tasks are not applicable to components with random characteristics of failure. It is a common trap for new reliability practitioners to attempt to implement preventive tasks on failure causes exhibiting random activity.

Consider the case of installing some protective bollards around a building or asset. The job of the bollard is to protect the building or asset when a vehicle loses control and veers toward it. The likelihood of vehicles hitting the bollards is random. When it occurs, the bollards are replaced with new ones. This situation is one of true random behavior, whereby it is quite easy to understand that there is no point replacing the bollard on a fixed interval, say, every six months.

A car could veer out of control and hit a bollard the day after it is installed or perhaps several months or years after it is installed. Its failure is not related to the age of the bollard, so any kind of preventive activity of fixed interval replacement is completely ineffective at preventing failure and simply adds extra cost.

So, before even considering if there is a preventive task that might be applicable, you first should establish if you have age related failure characteristics.

Predictive maintenance

The only option other than a preventive task is a predictive task. Predictive tasks are any type of task where its objective is to predict the onset of failure through detection of some alarm condition. Simple examples are feeling a bearing for excessive heat; listening to a bearing for excessive noise; or using sophisticated vibration spectrum analysis to determine increasing vibration levels. All of these inspections are designed to establish whether degradation has begun, thus predicting that a failure will occur at some time in the future.

Once the beginning of degradation has been detected, a future corrective action can be planned and executed so an unplanned failure event doesn't occur. This can mitigate the effect of unplanned outages on any production requirement or service level, plus it prevents any consequential damage that may occur if the item fails during operation. A simple example is changing a bearing once some level of degradation has been detected, rather than changing the whole shaft and bearing assembly if the bearing fails in service and destroys the shaft and housing.

Predictive tasks cover:
1. Sensory inspections (e.g., sight, sound, touch);
2. Condition monitoring (e.g., vibration, oil analysis, ultrasound);
3. Daily inspections;
4. Routine checks;
5. Measurements.

Essentially, predictive maintenance is any task where the objective is to establish the condition of the component or part. This is the basis of a predictive task; there is no actual maintenance activity, but rather an assessment of condition to predict the onset of failure.

Predictive tasks are applicable to all types of failure behavior. Even random failures may exhibit degradation that can be detected through a type of measurement or assessment so that the impending failure can be predicted and a corrective action executed. Of course, this is entirely dependent on the failure mode and cause.

It is here where the P-F interval becomes important. The P-F interval, which is the time interval between potential failure and functional failure, essentially describes how much time there is between when you can detect an impending failure and when it occurs.

For example, at some point in a bearing's life, it begins to degrade, depending on its duty, environment, operating condition, care, maintenance, etc. If you were to occasionally put your hand on the bearing while it was operating, you would begin to sense that the bearing is getting hotter and perhaps starting to vibrate. The point at which you detect that change is the potential failure point. Taking no action and letting the bearing run until it fails in service is a functional failure. The time between the potential failure and the functional failure is the P-F interval for this specific failure mode, for this specific component and for this specific inspection technique. The P-F interval, illustrated in Figure 14, shows the different inspection techniques or technologies that can detect the degradation at different stages. Thus, the P-F interval is dependent on not only the component and failure mode, but the inspection or monitoring technique employed.

It is important to recognize that the P-F interval is dependent on the failure mode and inspection technique and, in most cases, is not directly related to asset life. In other words, components with long lives can have short P-F intervals!

From a reliability strategy setting perspective, predictive tasks cover condition assessments that are completed on some interval, such

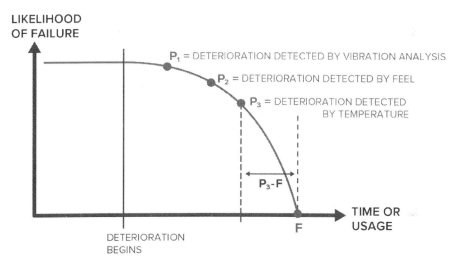

Figure 14: P-F interval for different techniques

as a weekly visual inspection for a specific degradation condition, but also cover continuous monitoring.

Online monitoring of asset condition is nothing more than a continuous predictive task. You are continuously monitoring for degradation of the asset. For example, you could conduct vibration analysis monthly on your critical assets, checking for vibration to go above some alarm point. If it's cost-effective, you could install some form of online, continuous vibration monitoring. Again, the intent is to alarm when the vibration hits set levels, indicating the component is deteriorating. The outcome is the same in both cases; if an alarm condition is met, then a corrective maintenance activity can be planned and executed.

Quantitative evaluation

The final step in determining the optimal maintenance strategy is the evaluation of the alternatives. It is critical that the total costs and risks are calculated for available alternatives so a comparison can be made.

Almost 60% of organizations use only a qualitative assessment of routine task effectiveness

For this to occur, it is necessary to specify relevant costs associated with all parameters in the calculation, such as the effects of failure, labor costs, material costs, unplanned repair costs, secondary action costs and, of course, the preventive or predictive task costs.

It is typical to use a Monte Carlo simulation, an accepted mathematical process, or an analytical approximation to generate the likely costs for each alternative over a set lifetime. This is repeated for all alternatives so they can be compared and the financially optimized task selected.

In cases where the effects of failure cannot be quantified into equivalent dollar terms, severity levels can be used. This leads to a comparison of cost and risk level for each alternative so the optimal task can be selected.

The ability to generate these quantitative evaluations of tasks is key to setting the optimal task in the first place, but critical to optimizing the tasks on an ongoing basis. It should be the goal that all future reliability strategy decisions are made based on real data. The ability to utilize the real data in a repeatable calculation becomes central to the improvement process.

Common traps

The most common misunderstandings by maintenance reliability professionals that produce significant reliability strategy setting errors are, without a doubt:

1. The use of MTBF to help set reliability strategy;
2. The lack of understanding the P-F interval, including how to use it.

Mean time between failures (MTBF)

MTBF is often used as a measure of performance. In its most simplistic sense, it gives an indication of the average life to be expected.

The problem is when the MTBF value is then used in setting the reliability strategy. What's not understood is that when using MTBF by default, you are describing an exponential distribution of failure. This means you are mathematically describing random failure as a constant failure rate. In others words, a probability of failure that does not change over time.

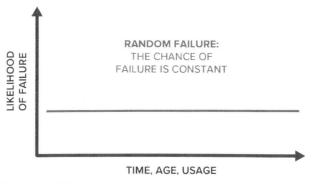

Figure 15: Random failure

Of course, the failure may, in fact, be a random failure, however, MTBF values are often used where aging is involved. If a component exhibits aging, its probability of failure increases with time.

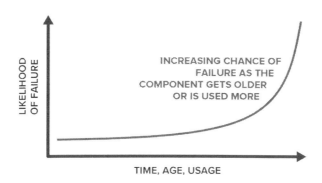

Figure 16: Age related failures

In these cases, the application of MTBF to support reliability strategy setting can led to erroneous results.

Consider these two extreme examples to illustrate the point:

Component A fails after ten hours. It's repaired and then fails after another one hundred and ninety hours of service. It's repaired again and then fails after another one hundred hours. Component A's MTBF is one hundred hours ((10+100+190)/3).

Component B fails after ninety-nine hours. It's repaired and then fails after another one hundred and one hours of service. It's repaired again and then fails after another one hundred hours. Component B's MTBF is one hundred hours ((99+100+101)/3).

Component A and Component B have the same MTBF. Is it likely you would consider the same reliability strategy for both? It is clear that Component B may be a good candidate for a fixed time change-out strategy before ninety-nine hours. Component A, however, appears much more random, with failure not seeming to correlate with age.

It is easy to see in this two examples that MTBF by itself doesn't present enough information about the characteristic of failure to support the reliability strategy setting process.

If you have any doubt over the value in using Weibull analysis, which is the most widely used distribution to describe equipment failure behavior, Component A and Component B should convince you of that value.

The other key element to understanding MTBF is that while it is easy to work from raw data, most people don't understand exactly what it means mathematically. Quite simply, if the MTBF is one year, this means the average life is one year and mathematically, sixty-three percent of items will have failed at one year! While there is no need to go into the mathematics for this book, suffice to say that characteristics of failure aside, using MTBF to set reliability strategy usually leads to erroneous results.

So, is MTBF of any use? Yes – MTBF is quite useful and effective at indicating if things are improving or deteriorating, particularly at an asset level. There is no harm in reporting on MTBF or, more effectively, the movement in MTBF of key assets to indicate if their performance is improving. However, MTBF is not useful in helping to optimize reliability strategy.

P-F interval

Although the P-F interval was discussed in the predictive maintenance section, it is relevant to cover here again as it remains one of the most widely misunderstood elements of setting effective reliability strategy.

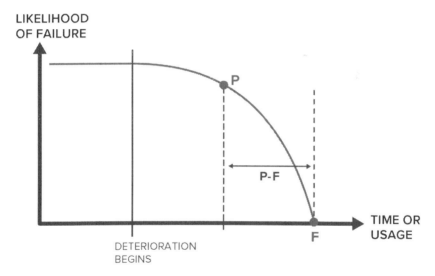

Figure 17: P-F interval

What's lacking is the practical application of the P-F interval. In many cases, the P-F interval is confused or combined somehow with the typical life of the component. It is critical to understand that P-F interval is not linked to the typical operational life of the component. In other words, a component may have an average life of twenty years and a P-F interval for a specific failure mode and inspection technique of twenty-four hours. On the other hand, a component may have an average life of one year and a P-F interval for a specific failure mode and inspection technique of one month.

It is key to recognize that:

1. The P-F interval is not related to component life;
2. The P-F interval is a characteristic of the degradation mechanism and the inspection technique/technology being considered;
3. The P-F interval supports the determination of the inspection or monitoring interval.

Several other variables make it complex to determine inspection or monitoring intervals without the use of a reliability calculator. The inspection interval is affected by:

1. Distribution or variability of the P-F interval;
2. The probability of the inspection or monitoring detecting the degradation condition when it is present;
3. The logistical ability to respond to an alarm condition and plan in a repair.

Several rules of thumb have been applied in terms of setting inspection intervals based on the P-F interval, such as half the P-F or one-third the P-F interval. However, in most cases, there is not enough real data to quantify the actual distribution of the P-F interval, yet it is a key element in setting inspection interval.

So, as a general guiding principle, when considering the P-F interval for any given component, failure mode and inspection technique, answer these questions:

1. Is the inspection currently being completed on this or a similar component? If so, are you still experiencing unplanned failures related to this failure cause, or did you catch them all?
2. When you completed the planned repair, what condition was the component in? Could it have operated longer or was it close to failure?

3. What do you believe is the shortest P-F practical for this failure mode and this inspection technique?
4. If you had one hundred of the same component, would the P-F be consistent or quite variable?

Using the answers to the above questions and any data that may be available, an assumed P-F interval needs to be determined to at least begin the reliability strategy setting process prior to being improved over time.

Of course, depending on the criticality of the asset and the impacts of failure, you may be conservative and apply some factors to ensure you err on the side of caution where risk is involved until data allows you to challenge the assumptions made.

The essential element to understand is that the P-F interval is used to set the interval of a predictive task. The predictive task interval must be less than the P-F interval, otherwise the component can go from no sign of degradation to failure between predictive tasks.

Other key considerations:

1. The P-F interval is not relevant for preventive tasks. A preventive task interval is set based on asset life, not the P-F interval.
2. The P-F interval does not typically change over the life of the asset. Beware of dangerous advice stating that if you have inspected a component a certain number of times, you can then extend the interval of the predictive task. This statement indicates a fundamental misunderstanding of the P-F interval and is evidence of it being confused somehow with asset life.
3. You must ensure the P-F interval being applied is relevant for the predictive task or technology in question. In general, technology-based tasks extend P-F intervals through greater ability to detect the early signs of degradation. For example, a vibration probe is more accurate at detecting increases in vibration than the human senses.

Implementation

Reliability strategy setting is simply not complete until it's implemented

The implementation part of any reliability strategy build or review project is to take the tasks identified, collect them into packages of work per the organization's agreed master data standards and complete the required master data so work packages can be loaded and made live in the EAM system.

This implementation process of asset reliability strategies has traditionally been the single biggest challenge for any structured reliability strategy review project, right behind getting the resources to conduct the project in the first place.

Over 80% of organizations report the implementation or update of maintenance plans generated from reliability strategy templates to be slow and manual

In most cases, implementing new or revised reliability strategies is equal in effort to the analysis project itself and, in almost all cases, isn't even considered when embarking on the project.

It is not surprising, then, that an alarming percentage of reliability strategy review projects simply don't get implemented at all, and those that do, once the tasks finally make it into the EAM system, there is not much resemblance to the output of the analysis.

Several key reasons make implementation challenging for most reliability strategy review projects:

1. The resources required for implementation are not considered as part of the analysis;
2. The leader of the reliability analysis does not have a sound understanding of the EAM system and relevant master data requirements;

3. The analysis and task interval setting may not consider the practical operations and shutdown cycle of the assets;
4. Key planning and EAM specialist resources do not have the right level of awareness and involvement in the analysis project;
5. The boundaries of the analysis are not consistent with the way maintenance plans are packaged within the EAM system;
6. There are no documented master data standards with the appropriate level of detail for consistent packaging of tasks into work plans.

With these elements in mind, the key is to develop an efficient implementation path before it is needed. Without the pressure of an impending project deadline and a sizable volume of data, clear heads can map and test the implementation path and address challenges as they arrive while also preempting other barriers that may arise with different data sets or packaging requirements.

Hence, a small pilot data set, as soon as available, should be taken and used to develop and test the implementation path. An ideal environment for successful implementation is:

1. Planning and relevant EAM system representatives are aware of and involved in the project as required.
2. The inclusion of implementation and required resources within the analysis project.
3. The use of master data standards (develop them if they are not available) that allow for rule-based packaging of work. This means tasks are grouped into maintenance plans based on rules, not expert opinion. This element is key for ensuring efficient and consistent grouping of tasks.
4. Electronically loading master data to the EAM system, if possible. Data should be translated directly from the reliability strategy development or review work without any requirement for someone to manipulate data, which, of course, provides a significant risk to data quality.

5. An understanding that your EAM system and master data standards and structure form part of your reliability engineers' competency so that they understand the practical manifestation of their reliability strategy decisions.

To really reduce the complexity and resources required for implementation, the two most important aspects are rule-based packaging of work to form the required master data and utilizing electronic data translation and input or update to the EAM system.

Over 70% of organizations report they do not have a consistent approach to structuring a maintenance plan's master data because it is manual

There are important aspects to consider when creating suitable master data standards. Most organizations have some master data standards, however, in most cases, they are not prescriptive enough to allow for rule-based packaging of work. In other words, they allow for some level of preference or opinion to influence how tasks are packaged in maintenance plans.

While a lack of rule-based packaging does not prevent implementation of the tasks, it does slow the process and supports fruitless debate. Ideally, the organization should develop master data standards to the point where rules can be used to package the work. At times, this can be challenging for experienced planners because there are several areas where it takes experience to make effective packaging decisions. In this case, it is a matter of extracting the logic used by the most experienced planner to make a decision that can be codified into rules.

The development of these packaging rules should be approached as an iterative process and one that continues for some time as all types of assets and plans are fed through the process. This iterative process ensures the rules are sound and provides a platform toward establishing a level of comfort in the output among the experienced planners and master data specialists.

SECTION 6
Asset Strategy Management (ASM)

Good reliability strategy is dynamic in a world of constant change

Having developed a new reliability strategy, or reviewed and optimized an existing one, and implemented it into the system, it is critical to manage the reliability strategy over time. The reliability strategies need constant refinement and adjustment to ensure they are always improving and delivering the optimal balance of risk, cost and performance, given the changing environment.

Asset strategy management is a dedicated process with the objective of ensuring reliability strategy decisions (i.e., what you choose to do) and strategy content (i.e., how you choose to do it and why) are optimal and implemented on all assets all the time. To ensure an optimal reliability strategy is on all assets all the time requires constant review and updates of asset performance and adjustment of the strategy to meet changing performance needs or operational conditions.

Asset strategy management is designed to manage the maintenance plans employed on an ongoing basis and provide the desired governance and control over a key element of asset performance. Like work execution management, ASM is a business process that describes how the maintenance plans are managed over time so they continue to provide the desired balance of risk, cost and performance. The process identifies trigger points to engage, accountabilities for analysis, review and approval and requires a technical solution to support the process. An ASM process delivers performance improvement on an ongoing basis, continually, as data becomes available.

While ASM and work execution management processes are connected, their differences are clear, based solely on their objectives.
- Work execution management is concerned with the effective and efficient management of work.
- Asset strategy management is concerned with ensuring ongoing governance and control over which maintenance plans are to be executed by the work execution management process.

A practical way to consider this is that a typical work planner deals with the work execution management process daily, while a site reliability engineer deals with the asset strategy management process daily.

Key elements to establish ASM

The four key pillars of ASM are:
1. Implement a management of change process for reliability strategy related content;
2. Implement a management system and process for reliability strategy content;
3. Implement reliability strategy review triggers;
4. Enable rapid deployment of reliability strategy updates.

These four key pillars are the basis to ensure that a sustainable strategy review and improvement process is in place and begins to gain traction in confirming the right reliability strategy is deployed to all assets.

Implement a management of change process for reliability strategy related content

The foundation of ASM within any organization is the management of change process for reliability strategy related content. To recap, reliability strategy related content includes anything related to the routine tasks you decide to do and how you plan to do them.

The defined process must contain the steps to be taken to:
1. Effect a change to the reliability strategy content, including the required review and approval;
2. Set clear roles and responsibilities for those involved in the process.

Typically, a process blueprinting exercise is completed to match the organization's structure, systems and objectives to a typical reliability strategy change management process. The process is then documented and readily available for reference.

It is common when mapping this process to constrain it to the reliability engineering aspect for successful implementation. However, to obtain full value, it is critical that a holistic approach is considered. At a minimum, the full process should involve asset managers, reliability leaders, maintenance leaders and planners and, perhaps, suppliers, stores, operations and corporate representatives.

For the ASM implementation to be successful, the process must support a nimble environment. Red tape must be at a minimum, with relevant review and approval only, and electronic management of the workflow, with escalation to ensure rapid movement of decisions through the process.

Part of ensuring the effectiveness of the process is making certain any reliability strategy content change is conducted using the process. Ultimately, there should be no changes to the reliability strategy content without application to the process. To this end, the EAM system should be locked down, if possible, so minimal resources can change the reliability strategy content and, in those cases, those users must be integral parts of the change process. Ideally, changes only should be made via a direct, electronic translation of data from the reliability strategy content management system.

SECTION 6

Implement a management system and process for reliability strategy content

To effectively implement a change management process, you need to establish how and where the reliability strategy content will be stored and managed. The system of choice must be able to support the process, store the data securely, allow access only to appropriate resources in the process, capture change logs and manage the content data over time.

To be successful, there needs to be one system for all reliability strategy related content for assets of all types and criticality. There are several instances where organizations have used different approaches for different criticality assets. While this may seem appropriate and can be effective, if it involves splitting data across different systems or files, the efficiency and accuracy will be significantly impacted.

It is also critical to note that EAM systems, by their very design, are not suitable for managing updates to the reliability strategy content over time. While they house the latest tasks to be executed and any information on how to execute them, they are not equipped to support reliability reviews, house the reliability analysis data, evaluate decisions, and capture a change log and justifications information. They also typically don't have a configurable workflow engine to support the reliability strategy change process.

Quite simply, this is not the intended function of EAM systems. They are in place to support the work execution management process and, in most cases, they have been set up very well to do that.

Several organizations have tried to either standardize or manage reliability strategy content within EAM systems and it became immediately apparent in all cases that the limitation far outweighs any benefit this approach may provide. In all cases, this effort was abandoned before even making it through a proof of concept stage.

While it may be possible to configure content management systems to support an ASM process to some degree, naturally an ASM solution is best positioned to support the process. With the right design intent and functionality, an ASM solution will drive discipline of the process, sophistication in the management of the content, and enormous efficiency and productivity gains in the reliability strategy management function.

Implement reliability strategy review triggers

A common question asked is, "How often should you review your reliability strategy?" The answer is, as often as you need to!

With a process established and a system in place, there is still no actual activity until the process is triggered. Setting process triggers is key for several reasons:

1. The process won't be used unless it is triggered;
2. The triggers decide when to work on what;
3. The triggers provide control over the volume of reliability strategy review work.

Most importantly, the triggers drive the application of resources by starting the process of review on a given asset. Of course, resources are valuable and not infinite, so you need to ensure they are focused in areas that deliver the most value.

Ultimately, if you have set your reliability strategy to deliver an agreed level of performance, there are three main reasons for review:

1. A failure has occurred and reoccurrence needs to be prevented;
2. Cases where you have several like assets, but different levels of performance;
3. Performance of an asset is much worse or better than forecasted (cost or reliability/availability).

The easiest trigger to establish and monitor is when a failure has occurred. In these cases, the failure itself is the trigger to the process. Generally, the trigger will be filtered so only failures on critical assets immediately trigger the process and/or the failure is over a certain cost or duration to rectify.

The second easiest trigger to implement is where there are like assets, but different levels of performance. This is dependent on the quality of the master data in the EAM system because you need to know the type of each asset in order to determine which assets are similar for the purpose of the comparison. Then, it is just a matter of comparing the performance data for similar assets and establish when there are deviations in performance great enough that warrant some review.

There are two ways to approach this:

1. Why are the assets performing the poorest performing worse than other similar assets?
2. Why are the assets performing the best performing so much better than other similar assets?

It is important to consider both approaches. In many cases, it could be a combination of how you are treating the poor performing assets versus the best performing assets that is resulting in the performance divide.

Finally, the most difficult trigger to establish, but usually the one that leads to the most improvement and puts the organization in a position of driving performance rather than being performance led, is identifying where performance is worse or better than forecasted.

To implement this trigger, the first step is to generate forecasted performance given to the implemented reliability strategies. Depending on the asset and the industry, the most common and basic metrics to forecast on are:

1. Cost;
2. Mean time to repair (MTTR);
3. MTBF;
4. Routine hours;
5. Interval compliance.

Essentially, you are looking for any area where the asset is not performing or being maintained as you would expect. Is the asset failing more than you forecasted? Is it costing more than forecasted? Is it taking longer to repair than forecasted? Are you spending more or less time on routine maintenance than forecasted? Is the actual interval of the planned activities greater than you set it to be?

The last metric is a critical one that currently goes unchecked and not considered in most organizations. It involves a simple check to determine the interval a routine activity is being completed. This is not what the system says it should be, but actually how often it has been performed. The accurate way to determine this is to simply look at the number of routine activities completed over a set calendar of time to establish the actual interval of execution.

Surprisingly, it is quite possible that a reliability strategy could be established, loaded and correctly set in the EAM system, but because of the way the EAM system is configured and the way the planning and scheduling process works, the actual interval is much different than what is set. This can lead to an organization running at extraordinary risk without knowing it or realizing significant performance issues. The reason, however, is hidden because the agreed reliability strategies are set in the EAM system.

Enable rapid deployment of reliability strategy updates

For an ASM process to take hold and deliver ongoing value, it must be easy to use. As per previous sections, one of the most challenging aspects of a reliability strategy update is implementing any new reliability strategies or changes to an existing reliability strategy. Hence, it is imperative that the implementation path is clear, efficient and accurate.

The implementation process has an element of management of change with respect to the work execution management team, so its involvement in the process is ideal. Ideally, this means team members will review and approve the actual master data changes prior to them getting implemented into the EAM system.

The goal is by the time the new or changed reliability strategies are in the EAM system, they are already understood and accepted by the work execution management team.

Several considerations support the implementation of an efficient deployment process:

1. As described in Section 5, rule-based packaging of master data; this drives consistency of output.
2. Effective comparison of current EAM system master data to the new master data that will be loaded for updates to the existing reliability strategies; this supports rapid review and understanding of the changes.
3. Remove the ability for changes to be made to the master data post-generation and prior to loading to the EAM system.
4. Create an electronic load process, where possible, to remove any errors that may be introduced through manually typing data.

In terms of ensuring good ownership, acceptance and contribution from planners and schedulers and EAM system administrators, the key aspect to tackle is ensuring that whatever is loaded or changed is more complete and/or better than what was there.

This might sound simple and, when just considering the reliability strategy content, it probably is. It becomes complex when more master data is added directly within the EAM system at some point to improve the master data quality or the planning and scheduling related content. It is important this content is not lost by being overwritten with an updated reliability strategy.

Whether this is even possible is dependent on the permissions and processes that are set to manage reliability strategy related content and associated master data. Where processes are implemented, and where it is possible, then it is a key consideration.

Some simple premises can help:

1. When comparing what is in the EAM system to what the proposed reliability strategy will be, use the actual data within the EAM system, rather than an archived snapshot of what was loaded in the past.
2. When conducting the comparison, only compare the reliability strategy related content so it is very clear what the differences are in the reliability strategy related data.
3. When updating existing reliability strategy, only overwrite the relevant related content fields.

In an ideal world, all the reliability strategy related content and related master data would reside in the system of choice to manage the strategy related content. Any changes to that content or related master data would be updated in that system prior to EAM system implementation. Thus, there is no concern that there may be updates in the EAM system that need to be incorporated into the reliability strategy update.

The three phases of ASM

ASM can be simplified into three main phases:

1. Build;
2. Deploy;
3. Govern.

Figure 18: Key aspects of the build, deploy and govern phases

Breaking down the process into these core elements, as shown in Figure 18, works for both an initial implementation and an ongoing ASM.

Build

The build phase covers setting the structure for reliability strategy and developing baseline, optimal reliability strategies for each equipment type for a given criticality.

Structured correctly, ASM offers a perfect platform for consolidating data and ensuring a single instance of each piece of reliability strategy content.

The first step is agreeing on the corporation's structured data for decisions.

1. Risk management framework
    a. Categories of risk
    b. Severity levels
    c. Likelihood levels
    d. Criticality levels or acceptable risk levels
2. Labor categories
3. Tools and equipment types
4. Code groups and structure
    a. Problem, Cause, Remedy
    b. Part, Cause, Damage
5. Materials

This data forms the basis of corporate data that will be used to compile the FMECA based reliability strategy decisions. The generation of this baseline reliability strategy data is the next step.

For example, when considering an electric motor, it doesn't really matter where it is installed or where it is within an asset or assembly. The underlying FMECA structure can be consistent, for the most part, given a set level of criticality. In other words, all the same failure modes will be present and all the potential tasks will be the same. It is the operational context that is likely to be altered if specific failure modes may occur, or at what likelihood. These differences will drive which tasks are relevant and at what interval.

What's important to understand here is that you want to utilize the same FMECA structure for electric motors, but just update the parameters based on operational, environmental, geographical, or any other context differences. What's most likely to change is the effects of failure, failure characteristics (e.g., estimate life not the type of failure) and task intervals, including being turned on or off.

With this mind-set, it becomes an efficient process to set up high quality FMECA structures and task lists for each asset type as a starting point for an organization. This can be done using some libraries or generic content, but it always should be compiled with current reliability strategies (e.g., for brownfield sites or for sites with a similar brownfield site) in mind.

Library content can be a time-saver, but you should not underestimate the knowledge that has been used to build existing plans within your EAM system. So, combining the two data sources usually leads to the best outcome.

The result is a baseline, best practices reliability strategy for each equipment type and for each level of criticality.

Deploy

One you have a baseline FMECA based reliability strategy for each asset type, you are ready to deploy the baseline reliability strategies to the actual asset listing of hierarchy.

Ideally, your master data is complete and you have identified equipment types within the EAM system. This significantly speeds up the assignment of the correct baseline reliability strategy to each asset.

There are four main components to deploy:

1. Use the baseline reliability strategies and account for any different operating context and environmental conditions.

2. Package the tasks into the agreed master data structure and implement to the EAM system.
3. Gather feedback of master data keys.
4. Forecast performance of the reliability strategy.

Using baseline reliability strategies

Making the baseline reflect the actual asset may require some local variations to the reliability strategy related data and/or content. For example, the baseline reliability strategy may record that the corrective task for a specific predictive task takes four hours to complete. At completion of the baseline strategy, the four hours assigned would represent a typical duration for that equipment type. However, in a specific case on an actual asset, the duration is more like eight hours because of the physical location of the asset.

This change represents a local variation, meaning a variation has been made to the reliability strategy based on local operating context or conditions.

It is important to note that only certain changes to the data constitute local variations and the underlying FMECA structure and potential task options should not need changing.

As an example, if there is a desire to add an additional failure mode that is not in the baseline reliability strategy, then this needs to be questioned before allowing the change. There are two possibilities:

1. The failure mode was missed or not understood at the time of creating the baseline reliability strategy. In this case, it should be included and any potential reliability strategy change considered on all instances of that equipment type.
2. The physical asset being considered requires an additional failure mode that does not belong in the baseline FMECA. This case is an indication that the specific asset is a different type, so a new baseline FMECA should be created for this type.

This might appear complex, however, it can be well controlled with a process that supports the continual development of the baseline reliability strategies and depth of types covered.

Packaging and generating master data

As covered in previous sections, once the reliability strategies have been reviewed and optimized as required based on local operating context and environmental conditions, the identified tasks are collected and structured into the appropriate master data structure.

The master data is then completed as per the agreed standards and implemented into the EAM systems. This might be via a load sheet that is then uploaded or, ideally, direct writing to the EAM system.

If the data is for updating existing reliability strategies for a brownfield site, then there is an extra step of direct comparison to what's currently in the EAM system so a change load sheet can be generated or the direct loading only changes the required parameters, rather than loading all new data.

In many cases, the agreed master data standards include the generation of the word processing software or file format documents, which are then attached to the plan structure within the EAM system. If this is the case, the documents provide a useful review tool for all stakeholders to review with when looking at new plans or changes to existing one.

Master data keys

To move into the govern stage of the ASM process, it is crucial that the master data keys for the loading of any new master data plan structures is loaded to the reliability strategy content management system.

In other words, if new master data is loaded, at some point, the new maintenance plans are assigned a plan number. This key, which is a unique plan number, provides a way to identify that plan alone and needs to be recorded against the reliability strategy content. This is a critical step and must form part of the strategy content management system's capability so that the connection between reliability strategy content and the EAM system's master data is created.

This connection then provides a link to support any future reliability strategy content updates and enables efficient updates and changes of any existing reliability strategies as they get reviewed in the future.

Forecasting reliability strategy performance

Depending on the level of data included within the baseline content and the level of review for local variations, it may be possible with this available data to generate performance predictions or forecasts about how the reliability strategy will perform.

If financial optimization of the reliability strategies occurred during the baseline reliability strategy stage, there will be enough data to support the forecasting. It is a worthwhile step since true strategy review triggers can be put into place.

In the absence of performance forecasting, triggers are limited and tend to just focus on the worst performing assets. While these are legitimate triggers for review, they tend not to change over time and they prevent other assets that could be improved from being reviewed.

The point here is that your high cost assets tend to always be your high cost assets and there are diminishing returns over time when addressing them. On the other hand, there may be several assets just off the top ten charts that are costing one hundred percent more than they should, but because they are not on the top ten, they don't get reviewed.

The type of information that can be forecasted and support triggers is:

- Cost;
- MTBF;
- MTTR;
- Routine hours per year.

This information allows you to establish, for example, whether you are spending more hours on routine maintenance than forecasted. It may not show up as one of the top costs, but certainly provides a point of review and a potential area for savings.

If MTBF is lower than forecast, this also may be on an asset where costs don't show up in the top ten, but if the asset's failure is much more than forecasted, it should be reviewed to address the issue.

Governance

Now that the reliability strategies have been deployed, another key aspect of the ASM process is to drive governance. Governance of asset reliability strategies assures compliance and drives continuous improvement of the maintenance plans employed on all assets.

Continuous improvement

It can be typical for organizations to be in a position whereby:

1. Master data structures are inconsistent;
2. Identifying the entire approved maintenance plans on any specific asset is difficult;
3. Identifying whether the maintenance plans currently in the EAM system match the approved maintenance plans is challenging;
4. Identifying what risks maintenance plans carry, if any, is needed due to their inconsistent execution in the EAM system.

An asset strategy management process addresses all these issues through a governance process driven by formal workflows.

It is not uncommon for work management practices, which take account of resource constraints and work priorities, that the interval when a specific task is carried out is greater than the specified and agreed interval. It is also not uncommon for the interval within the EAM system for a given task to be different from the agreed interval simply through unreviewed, uncontrolled changes. Both issues can lead to significant risk.

What's required is the implementation of a reliability strategy change process, as described earlier in this section, and ensuring no available work-arounds.

Constant monitoring of the alignment of reliability strategy to actual work is paramount. Like all areas of monitoring and improvement, focusing efforts on the key areas will drive success.

The triggers for review, as discussed earlier in this section, ensure that the review and improve process is triggered. Provided that the reliability strategy review is conducted with the key principles of reliability strategy review in mind and by a suitably trained resource, continuous improvement will take care of itself.

If all the elements have been implemented:

1. Reliability strategy content can be changed only by approved resources.
2. A structured review and approval process has been implemented.
3. There is a path to implement any reliability strategy changes into the EAM system.
4. There are sound triggers that trigger the process to begin and focus resources on the areas where maximum improvement can be made.

Then, a continual loop of improvement is established. The continuous improvement loop takes care of ensuring that the reliability strategies you have deployed are delivering the performance you require.

Compliance

In an ideal world, ensuring compliance is as simple as ensuring only people with appropriate training, expertise and the applicable role in the organization can change reliability strategy related content.

But, the environment most of us operate in is a bit away from the ideal world! Even in organizations that have locked down authorities and constrained who can change reliability strategy related data within their EAM systems, there are generally work-arounds or it has been constrained to master data experts rather than reliability strategy experts, so the accountability for what data is changed is not clear.

So, assessing compliance to the approved reliability strategies is an ongoing exercise. This should be continuously monitored and represented on a simple chart displaying risk levels.

If the reliability strategy development or review work has been completed to the appropriate level of detail, then all the information will be available to determine risk levels for various scenarios.

For example, if the reliability strategy review determines an interval should be four weeks, then there are two levels of assessment to check for compliance:

1. What is the interval that is recorded within the EAM system?
2. Regardless of what interval is recorded within the system, what interval is the activity being completed at?

These two assessments are important because, generally, there are several items where intervals have changed for some reason and they no longer match the agreed reliability strategy. Let's say the four week interval has been changed to six weeks to line up with some operational cycle. So, within the EAM system, you can see that the interval assigned to the plan is now six weeks and a clear deviation from the four weeks strategy decision.

At this point, you can assess what that means in terms of increased risk by using all the parameters established to optimize the reliability strategy in the first place. The impacts of failure and other key information, such as failure characteristics and P-F intervals, if applicable, would have been defined.

The second assessment picks up normally hidden risk. This is where the interval recorded against the item in the EAM system is four weeks, so, on the surface, it appears there is compliance with the set reliability strategy. However, you look at actual history and see that only eight inspections have been completed over the last twelve months. This, of course, can happen for various reasons and may even be the result of the WEM process that was applied. In this case, the effective interval is, in fact, around six weeks. Again, you can calculate the risk exposure for completing the activity at six weeks compared to the optimized interval of four weeks.

Figure 19: Increasing risk based on reliability strategy content changes

Figure 19 shows how an organization may carry different and likely unknown undesirable levels of risk, depending on the level of governance they have.

This risk-based assessment of compliance drives attention to the areas of noncompliance that are yielding the highest risk and should be addressed as a matter of priority.

Most organizations are likely carrying significant risk through a combination of both mechanisms, where the interval does not match the approved reliability strategy.

SECTION 7
ASM and Asset Performance Management (APM)

Monitoring performance of assets does not remove the need for reliability strategy; Reliability strategy delivers the performance that's being monitored!

What is APM?

Asset performance management is a broad term and remains somewhat undefined within the asset management community. For the most part, it is a term used when describing ongoing condition monitoring and assessment of an asset's condition or health.

This book defines APM as the continuous monitoring of asset performance data, with the intent of identifying impending failures, thereby allowing intervention in a planned manner.

A simple example is the online, continuous monitoring of vibration levels of a bearing. When the vibration hits a preset high vibration level, an alarm is triggered and, most likely, a work order is triggered to investigate the cause.

It is very important to discern that APM is concerned with monitoring performance, assessing equipment condition, detecting some deterioration and looking for some sign of an impending failure.

APM, therefore, is simply an advancement of predictive type tasks. Simple predictive tasks are sensory based inspections, such as visual checks. More advanced predictive tasks are, for example, periodic vibration analysis, where every month a technician conducts a vibration reading and the results are trended over time to support the detection of any deterioration. Then, these tasks progress to online vibration monitoring and alarms.

An APM program, then, is the collection of online, continuous monitoring asset performance related data, such as vibration, temperature, noise levels and oil quality.

Advancements in technology have supported the growth of APM programs because the cost of online sensors have decreased significantly, while the ability to connect them remotely to either local networks or cloud-based systems has also improved.

The Industrial Internet of Things (IIoT) has gained much hype through the cost-effective nature of allowing sensors to be connected via existing infrastructure. The proliferation of connected devices and sensors provides an abundance of data.

Enter big data, meaning the ability to support extremely large data sets, which may be from IIoT based devices and other relevant data sources, for the purpose of being analyzed computationally.

The intent is to reveal trends, associations, or patterns that can then, in this case, support better detection of deterioration and drive better interventions.

Ideally, this technology will not only use the available data for prognostics (i.e., advanced indication of an impending failure), but also for diagnostics (i.e., identification of the actual cause of the impending failure).

This computation analysis is often referred to as machine learning, deep learning, or pattern recognition. All have a specific meaning, however, the intent is basically to have the analysis learn through experience what is happening to the asset, given the current assessment provided by each individual sensor or device.

For example, the temperature has risen five degrees, the sound has increased 3dB, the electrical current has increased two percent, all typically mean the lubrication is breaking down and action needs to be taken.

The concept is intriguing and has been proven in a small number of cases. It is expected that this area will continue to develop and add value to the asset management process.

Currently, not all known modes of failure can be monitored. However, even if you could monitor for all failure modes, then the entire APM process is predictive in nature and not a substitute for reliability strategy. Essentially, APM provides a technology-driven predictive function.

When setting a reliability strategy, there are two task types to choose from: preventive and predictive. A reliability strategy setting then can be used to determine where APM is cost-effective to apply, given that it is a technology-driven predictive function that amounts to a continuous assessment of condition and one where, as technology continues to improve, may support more advanced notice of impending failures. Furthermore, it may support in determining the actual causes of deterioration, thus speeding up rectification and providing the data to support reliability strategy improvement.

Assessment of areas where APM yields sound return on investment is important. While the concept of machine learning based algorithms to determine impending failures and causes is intriguing, to date, it is costly to develop these models, simply because the model is unique to each asset in each installation. As such, the learning process, which requires significant support in the first instance, is a critical, resource-intensive one.

In most cases, APM implementation may start with plans for multivariant, algorithm-based predictions, but organizations largely resort to single parameters monitoring and alarm functionality. Of course, this still can add enormous value through cost-effective and constant prediction of impending failures.

ASM and APM – Which comes first?

Once understanding the clear difference between ASM and APM, a common question is: Which comes first? The answer, from a theoretical perspective, is that implementing ASM first will support the development of the APM requirement and establish the value and cost benefit of such a system.

This is simply due to the evaluation of the reliability strategy setting or the review of the most cost-effective task, preventive or predictive. Several different predictive tasks can be considered to find the optimal approach. This could be from manual visual inspections at some frequency to implementation of continuous online monitoring and a full APM solution.

In an organization with neither APM nor ASM, ASM should be implemented first and then APM where it is deemed cost-effective. It is also possible to grow the APM approach over time as more and more advanced predictive technology is implemented across the site or organization.

The reality is that most existing sites have varying levels of APM in place, even if they don't call it APM and don't have a single dedicated system to complete the monitoring and management of the data and process. In these instances, implementing ASM is no different in sites where all current predictive tasks are routine based. The ASM implementation simply accounts for all current predictive activity, routine based or continuous.

Delivering performance with WEM, APM and ASM

World-class performance will be delivered when the asset management environment includes WEM, APM and ASM best practices working together.

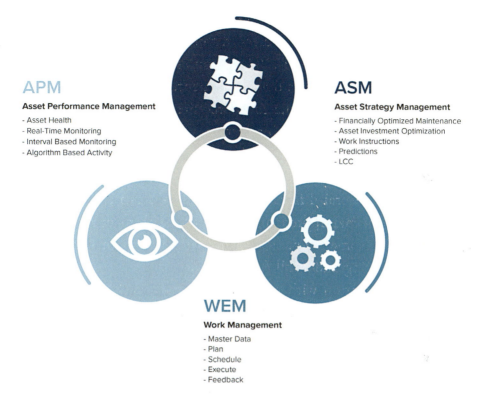

Figure 20: World-class asset management framework

All three elements are essential for world-class performance:

- ASM – Ensures the best reliability strategies are on all assets at all times;
- APM – Predicts impending failures supporting maximum life and reduction in unplanned failures;
- WEM – Ensures efficient execution of work and capture of data so ASM and APM can drive performance improvement.

All three elements are generally supported by an enterprise level technical solution. This ensures compliance to the process and consistency of application.

There are natural data connections and flow of data between the three elements that should be electronic and live where possible.

What is critical, however, is defining the master process and technical solution for each piece of connected data.

From an ASM perspective, any data element that is considered reliability strategy content must be considered the master within the ASM technical solution. In other words, the ASM technical solution is the master system for the interval field of maintenance plans. This data element appears within the EAM system as content on that maintenance plan, but this should not be considered the data master and, therefore, should not be changed within the EAM system. If there is a discrepancy between the field in the EAM system and the ASM system, then the data should be pushed from the ASM system into the EAM system to resynchronize the data.

At a high level, the connection between the systems are:

- ASM-WEM: Reliability strategy related content is implemented to the EAM system. Work order history and performance data is read from the EAM system and used to drive the review in the ASM system. Updated reliability strategies will be implemented into the EAM system.
- ASM-APM: ASM identifies areas for APM implementation. APM data is read by the ASM system to support reliability strategy review and performance forecasting.
- APM-WEM: APM creates work requests in the EAM system to initiate interventions and prevent unplanned failures. Some data may be read from the EAM system to support asset condition assessment.

All three elements can be established, improved and made more sophisticated over time. Since the first step of ASM is to build and then deploy reliability strategy, these early steps of ASM should be completed first. Then, WEM can be established or improved to support execution of the reliability strategies. An element of APM may be established at the same time if the reliability strategy determines online continuous monitoring is applicable.

With all three elements established to certain degrees, they all can be escalated over time. There is no doubt that the return on investment for ensuring that the reliability strategy is up-to-date will support the establishment of the governance element of ASM as soon as possible and ensure appropriate resources are in place.

SECTION 8

ASM and Big Data, Digital Transformation and IIoT

Big data and digital transformation (alone) will not deliver reliability

Digital transformation in asset management

Section 7 covered how IIoT and big data contribute to APM. Of course, they both impact asset management, in general. While there is much hype surrounding digital transformation, IIoT and big data, in most cases, the actual meaning is not well understood.

Digital transformation is a significant transformation of an organization to leverage the value provided through a mix of digital technologies. From an asset management perspective, the impact is relatively clear with advancements in EAM systems, mobility, augmented and virtual reality, predictive technologies, computational analysis capabilities and database advancements.

IIoT and big data are more specific, with IIoT referring to the proliferation of Internet connected devices. Technology advancements, coupled with the cost (which has reduced significantly) of supplying or implementing connected devices and sensors, have created the ability for most assets to be connected in some way.

Big data simply refers to the capability to create enormous data sets for computational analysis. Two advancements have led to the concept of big data. The first is the technical capability of computer systems to store, manipulate and provide ways to view and interpret vast sets of data. The second is the advancement of analysis techniques, such as pattern learning and deep learning. These analysis techniques basically enable the determination of complex associations that may be apparent within the data, but simply are not detectable by data analysts who just mine the data.

It is, of course, the patterns that provide the ability to then create a model that can forecast likely outcomes based on multivariant inputs.

If you take the traditional P-F curve, the more sophisticated the inspection technique, the further back on the degradation curve the impending failure is, which basically translates to a greater warning of an impending failure and more time to manage the required intervention.

More advanced models can be developed with pattern recognition and deep learning, which means if operational and environmental parameters are included in the analysis, you may be able to detect conditions that lead to degradation. The point is there is opportunity to plan an intervention that may not involve an asset repair or replacement, but may be a process or operational change, meaning the asset doesn't even start to deteriorate at that point.

This can be simply thought of as moving even further back on the P-F curve, so far, in fact, that the intervention required has changed from an asset repair/replacement to another change that prevents the actual degradation from starting.

The theory is sound, but in practice, there are several challenges. The development of these models is key to the successful application of the technology. Given that the models involve asset, operational and environmental parameters, it is not difficult to see that the models for each asset in each operation is unique. This translates to an enormous effort for each implementation to determine, refine and validate the model on every asset.

From an ASM perspective, these advancements in detection of degradation or future degradation are only positive in terms of providing alternate reliability strategies to manage assets. ASM supports the determination of where this approach is cost-effective and helps drive the application of the technology where it adds most value.

It is also important to appreciate that even a futuristic site, where every asset and every potential failure mode is monitored, which, of course, is not currently a realistic option, would still require ASM to manage the reliability strategy and reliability strategy related content.

Even with all the sophisticated monitoring, at some point the practicalities of asset maintenance comes into play:

1. If monitoring determines an intervention is required, what else should be maintained while the asset is getting attention?
2. At what point is it best to replace the entire asset?
3. Is there a place for some fixed time repairs/replacements to ensure the asset runs for the next mission time or run time and, if so, when are they done?
4. How should you manage interventions to smooth resource profiles and manage any logistical constraints?
5. When an intervention is called for, what is the activity that needs to be executed and how is that activity performed? This constitutes the reliability strategy content and must continually be improved and updated.

IIoT and big data also have wider implications on asset management and, in particular, ASM.

Where's the big data?

Big data is all around. As EAM systems mature, they begin to capture staggering amounts of data. APM solutions or even basic condition monitoring systems collect this data. Any system that is capturing real-time data, of course, generates large volumes of data every day.

Essentially, then, combining all the relevant data sources into large data sets gives rise to the term, big data or these almost inconceivable sets of data.

From an asset management and ASM perspective, these big data sets allow for the analysis of assets based on all available parameters.

Imagine looking at data relating to assets of a specific type and being able to interrogate all the work completed, by whom, when what else operationally was going on, material movements, resources doing the work, asset condition information, process or operational conditions and parameters.

To derive any intelligence, of course, requires very sophisticated data mining skills. However, the ability to draw conclusions from analyses showing relationships between different data elements supports much more informed decision-making.

What can big data really do for you?

From an ASM perspective, data is key for two elements:

1. Reliability strategy review;
2. Triggering reliability strategy review.

Reliability strategy review

Effective reliability strategy review is underpinned by accuracy of:

1. Failure impacts;
2. Failure characteristics;
3. Task information (e.g., duration, resources, materials);
4. P-F intervals.

To conduct reliability strategy development before the asset is in service requires assumptions to be used as a basis for the decision-making. When a reliability strategy is reviewed, in many cases, accurate data is still difficult to obtain. So, it's usually a case of using some data coupled with experience-based assumptions to support the decision-making.

The real opportunity, then, is to utilize big data sets and more advanced computational analytics to determine with greater accuracy the key variables.

As data quality improves, the data set gets larger, then the analysis likely gets more specific. You should get to the point where the accuracy of the key variables for each asset is such that the decision-making takes simple math to determine the optimal reliability strategies.

It is also possible and likely that real-time changes to the reliability strategy are possible for every asset, solely based on the insight gained from the analysis of its unique data set.

Triggering reliability strategy review

As discussed in previous sections, reliability strategy review should be triggered based on data analysis. Essentially, you are looking for areas of high cost or poor performance, but you are also concerned with assets that are simply not performing as you would like. It could be you are spending more or less planned hours than you should, or costs are higher or lower than expected. Both provide good areas to make potential cost savings and/or performance gains.

Big data can support this analysis through the incorporation of other data sets, not just EAM data, into the assessment. There may be an apparent deviation from forecasted expectations when considering EAM data only, but coupled with operational data, you can see the change really is with operations and not the asset. Of course, this in itself may warrant a reliability strategy adjustment, however, it must be made clear on what basis.

As the concept of big data takes hold in organizations, the available connected data set will allow for more sophisticated and advanced triggering of which reliability strategies to review.

ASM and big data

Thus far, this section has covered the use of IIoT and big data to support ASM. Of course, it should be noted that all ASM data should become part of the big data set itself.

Reliability strategy related data and content is an important element to the asset's data and will provide additional variables to consider when looking for behavior patterns to drive improvement.

Hence, any technical solution supporting ASM should have open architecture, while continuing to be the system of record for key reliability strategy data and content.

Going digital with ASM

When implementing ASM, there is an opportunity to step into a digital implementation or go digital from the start. ASM should be based on digital reliability strategies; this content is the reliability strategy element of a digital twin. It can be used to forecast the performance of the asset, given the implementation of the reliability strategy, and in the stated operational context.

The benefit is the ability to create reliability strategy scenarios and establish the likely performance changes and risk positions.

For example, you may model the impact of extending shutdown intervals, extending inspection intervals or condition assessment tasks, or changing the reliability strategy while supporting operations with some form of redundancy of work-around.

The use of a digital reliability strategy supports continuous improvement through exploration in a digital environment prior to implementation. Given that the digital reliability strategy can predict performance, it also can be used to understand key or critical elements.

Suppose you establish a reliability strategy scenario where you extend a shutdown interval, but the result is risk and cost increases because the components currently are not predicted to make the required life extension. The digital reliability strategy can be used to determine exactly which components are key to improve so that the interval extension becomes viable.

The value and leverage provided by going digital with ASM make reliability strategy management not only possible, but a simple and efficient process. Going digital supports the full value delivered through actual data-driven insights and logic-derived recommendations for implementation

SECTION 9

ASM, Asset Management Systems and the Uptime Elements

It is useful to consider how ASM connects with or interacts with the wider asset management system. With the uptake of ISO55000 in many organizations, there is great emphasis on establishing an asset management system. An asset management system should be viewed as a holistic approach to direct, coordinate and control asset management activities and deliver the objectives of the organization.

It is stated in ISO55000 that "effective control and governance of assets by organizations is essential to realize value through managing risk and opportunity in order to achieve the desired balance of cost, risk and performance."

This single statement connects the asset management system to the requirement for ASM because you cannot have effective control and governance of your assets if there is no governance and control of your asset reliability strategies.

What's clear is that ASM exists within the asset management system, so using an established framework ensures alignment of the organization and supports continued development of both ASM and the asset management system.

The Uptime® Elements™ A Reliability Framework and Asset Management System™ was developed by Reliabilityweb.com to align with ISO55000. What's more, the Uptime Elements provides a much needed layer of detail and, most importantly, a common language and framework that allows the connection of colloquial language used within a site or organization to the wider asset management community and network.

Many frameworks are available, however, the Uptime Elements treads the line between a dogmatic rigid framework and a nimble, flexible framework. The Uptime Elements provides a pragmatic framework that is clear in the disciplines and elements within each discipline, the terminology that is appropriate and associated definitions.

The benefit of this consistent language supports the advancement of the asset management discipline within any organization, specifically through the development of reliability leadership and reliability for everyone.

ASM, Asset Management Systems and the Uptime Elements

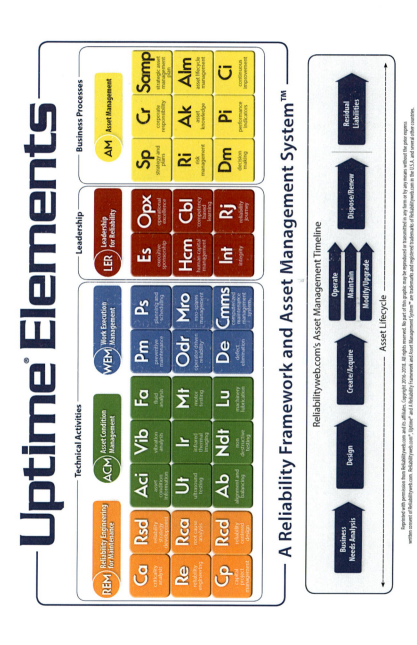

Figure 21: The Uptime Elements

Successfully implementing ASM into an organization should include both embedding a process and supporting it with education, training and awareness to underpin a change in the organization's reliability culture and reframe the approach to improving asset performance through asset strategy management.

The connection between ASM and the Uptime Elements is the language framework and the way in which each of the relevant elements connect through the ASM process. These same elements connect to the entire asset management system and the approach to reliability leadership.

Where an organization chooses to align to the Uptime Elements an ASM implementation presents an opportunity to begin or continue the establishment of the Uptime Elements framework by using consistent language and terminology. Then, the approach to reliability leadership can support the wider uptake of both ASM and the Uptime Elements framework within the asset management discipline.

SECTION 10

ASMx – Connected Digital Reliability Strategies

ASMx – going digital with ASM, efficiently delivering and governing effective reliability strategy

ASMx is one approach to ASM that has been developed and refined in recent years to best utilize the latest technology. The key differentiators of ASMx ensure the ASM process will be sustained and deliver maximum return on investment (ROI) for the reliability function.

ASMx is focussed on improving a typical approach to ASM by addressing the following main challenges:

1. Difficulty in maintaining and reducing duplicate data;
2. Difficulty in applying generic content while allowing unique differences;
3. Difficulty in implementation of reliability strategies;
4. Difficulty in making the review and improvement process work and take hold.

With those challenges in mind, the key design principles of ASMx are:

1. Consolidate data through the use of the design principle that data only appears once and is replicated wherever it is used;
2. The use of generic data, but allows for variations;
3. Automated, rule-based task grouping, packaging, structuring and completely ready for import;
4. Defined, automatic workflows that create adherence to the process;
5. Automatic triggers for the process.

Consolidating data

Data consolidation is required to drive consistency across the reliability strategy content and associated master data. For years, localization of data has been tolerated, but, in most cases, added no benefit.

The challenge with data consolidation is determining the level at which to apply the consolidation. If you consider an asset as a collection of components, it is easy to see that if you consolidate data at an asset level, all the pump sets and blower assemblies, for example, may be consistent. However, a particular motor that is common across both the pump sets and blower assemblies looks different in each because the standardization has occurred at too high of a level.

The best starting point for ensuring consistency from a reliability strategy perspective is to consider the underlying FMECA. The FMECA should be at a component level. As a general guide, a component is a collection of parts. One FMECA should be then used to cover all components that have the same failure modes.

ASMx then allows for overrides to be placed on the FMECA structure to represent different criticalities, operating contexts, and makes and models.

For example, a standard electric induction motor should have consistent failure modes and potential tasks. The ASMx process then allows for overrides to occur to the FMECA, which may change task intervals, including enabling or disabling the task. Failure characteristics may change, which subsequently may change task intervals or materials associated with the tasks for specific makes and models of the component.

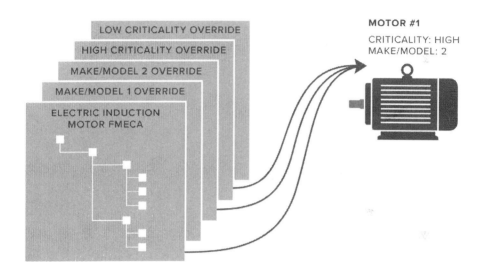

Figure 22: Generic FMECA with overrides

The concept here is to allow the management of a single FMECA, where relevant, to represent a component. Then, when that FMECA is applied to an actual asset, as shown in Figure 22, there may be several overrides to the reliability strategy data related to the operating context, criticality, and make and model of the component.

With consolidated FMECAs in place, you can take data consolidation and the use of generic content down to the next level and standardize the failure mode, cause coding or descriptions, and task descriptions.

This process of data consolidation allows for a single data element to be used wherever applicable, which, in turn, drives enormous productivity with the reliability function. This concept means that a single task description, such as conducting vibration analysis, taking an oil sample, or calibrating common devices, can be written once and deployed to all plans where it is relevant, as illustrated in Figure 23.

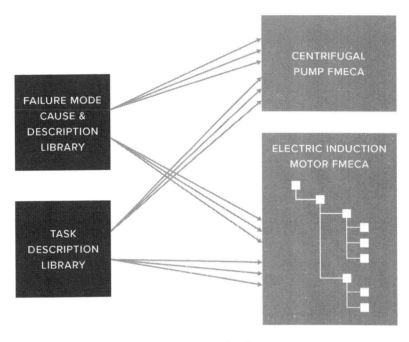

Figure 23: Using generic cause and task phrases

The advantage is a transformational step in consistency, but also a clear improvement path, whereby if the phrase needs to be modified, it can be changed once and deployed wherever used.

Managing variations

While standardization drives simplicity, consistency and productivity, the limitation of standardization is the ability to reflect the individual nature of assets and their related operational context and associated maintenance plans.

ASMx allows for group or local variations to be made without losing the connectivity back to the consolidated data set. This sophisticated connected data set is a key foundational principle that moves

ASMx beyond an analog ASM process and into a digital connected environment.

Returning to the example of the typical electric induction motor, which has a generic FMECA structure, along with some recorded overrides, based on the criticality of the asset the motor is part of and some cataloged materials from a specific make and model of that motor type. When connected to an actual asset in the asset list, given that you know the make and model of that motor and the criticality of the asset, the connection allows for the FMECA structure and associated reliability strategy to be based on the criticality and make and model.

Now, you can create any variations required to ensure the reliability strategy is specific to this actual asset. This may include parameters, such as repair times, resource assignments, equipment requirements and task durations. It may even include variations to the failure characteristics and tasks and their intervals. However, to make any generic content specific to an asset, be aware that a small percentage of all the input data is made specific. The flip side, of course, is that most of the data remains the same as the generic content.

The benefit is that any changes to the generic component type content flows through to any asset where that content has been connected. If variations have been made, they will be ignored and only generic content will be updated.

The concept of variations can be considered for both groups of assets or local to just one asset.

Group variations

Imagine the generic electric induction motor FMECA structure and its associated reliability strategy content is used within a multinational organization. In cases like this, it is common for regional or site-based changes to be made to the generic content to reflect variations that are consistent across a geographical region or specific site.

These could include resource assignment changes, such as different trade classifications or resource capabilities split in different ways in different regions.

They also could be predictive task changes based on the maturity of the site or logistical challenges in making a specific technology available at that site.

The benefit of group variations is that only one change needs to be made to reflect any variation that is consistent across all instances of that component type.

Local variations

Local variations are any required changes to the reliability strategy content to ensure the assigned FMECA and related content matches the specific asset. Typically, these changes are related to task durations and task intervals based on operational and environmental context.

What's not a variation

It's important to understand what parameters should not be changed or regarded as a variation. For example, if you want to add in additional failure modes to the underlying FMECA structure, this can only mean one of two possibilities:

1. The failure mode was missed as a potential failure mode of this component type and, therefore, should be added to the generic content;
2. This is a different component requiring a different FMECA structure.

This concept is in alignment with the guideline that components are of the same type if their underlying FMECA is the same.

By the same token, neither failure mode descriptions nor task descriptions should be changed. This ensures that consistency remains with the fundamental FMECA structure.

Variation reporting

As with most elements of the ASM process and the review and approval process, it is critical that the processes are matched to the organization, its structure and resources. In ASMx, variation reporting is a critical element, allowing for variations across the asset base to be assessed at all times.

At any point in time, the difference between a reliability strategy for a specific asset and the underlying generic FMECA and generic content should be available.

This variation reporting is important to ensure compliance can be managed irrespective of the review and approval process being applied.

It also supports continuous improvement by allowing an assessment of changes to be made to any asset that is performing better than the forecast or, in comparison, to like component types across the asset base.

Task packaging into work plans

ASM is based around a logic-based, rule-driven packaging process. The packaging of tasks into an agreed maintenance plan structure is critical for successful implementation of either new or revised reliability strategies.

With ASMx, automatic packaging completely removes any manual grouping of tasks. This leads to significant productivity improvement because plan structures can be created and assessed, content changed, then regrouped and checked again, in a desktop environment prior to implementation.

Like variations made to the reliability strategy content when applied to an actual asset, manual updates to rule-based content may be necessary for very specific plans.

Following appropriate investigation, rules should be developed to support any manual decision-making process, except for subjective decision-making, which should be avoided at all costs. However, in the early stages of the change management process, this can be quite challenging to traditional plan structuring processes, so some flexibility may be allowed.

In cases where package overrides are allowed, they should be stored and not updated when the automatic packaging runs again. The intent of automatic packaging is to engage the planning and EAM system representatives in the ASM process and ensure the complete reliability strategy management approach is holistic, yet separated from the WEM process.

Automatic packaging, especially if completely rule-based with no allowance for overrides, is another element of driving uncompromised consistency of maintenance plans related to master data content.

Workflows

ASMx is centered on configurable workflows that support ASM within each individual organization and site. It is imperative for success that the workflows are set to support the resources available within the organization.

For large organizations, the structure and resources are often already in place and aligned to support central governance of reliability strategies and local variations, packaging and implementation at a site level. For example, an organization may have a corporate reliability group that is accountable for corporate baseline reliability strategies. They likely have reliability engineers in place who are accountable for local variations to the reliability strategies and site-based planners who ensure compliance to the packaging framework and support implementation.

In smaller organizations or organizations with no central reliability function or group, a matrix style approach is typically used.

For example, an experienced rotating equipment expert on one site may be used as a group subject matter expert for rotating equipment and be accountable for any updates to the agreed upon central baseline reliability strategies. On another site, an experienced air compressor expert may be accountable for all air compressor related baseline reliability strategies across the group.

Either way, what's required is a workflow structure that ensures an appropriate review and approval of relevant changes from work packages to local variations and baseline reliability strategies.

ASM process triggers

No process is used or followed unless it is triggered in some way. The ASMx approach has very prescriptive triggers to ensure a review is conducted where it adds the most value and confirms compliance to the corporation's risk appetite.

The use of digital reliability strategy content generates forecasts of expected performance, costs and resource usage. A comparison of actual performance, costs and resource usage against the forecasts delivers insight into areas clearly not behaving as forecasted and expected. Reviewing these areas allows for optimization of the reliability strategies in alignment with the latest data. The outcome can result in reduced cost or risk, depending on the area or difference.

The ability to forecast performance, risk and costs also allows a forecast of predicted performance based on current and actual routine task cadence. Take, for example, a reliability strategy that identifies some tasks that should be completed every month, but using actual history, it is determined the activity is being completed once every six weeks. This may be exposing the organization to unacceptable risk. Identifying these areas prior to any undesirable event occurring allows for correction and management of risk to within acceptable risk levels.

Leveraging value with ASMx

It is the combination of the key design principles of ASMx that provide value, both in terms of the productivity of the reliability function and the ability to leverage key learnings and improvements across an entire organization.

Productivity

With the ability to manage reliability strategy review, approval and updates with digital workflows, plus digital reliability strategy content and rule-based task packaging and implementation, productivity gains to an organization are significant.

The concept of keeping reliability strategies aligned to the current operating environment becomes automatic, dynamic and efficient. Most of all, it leads to a true data-driven decision-making environment.

Fundamentally, the time taken to review a reliability strategy, which includes understanding the current reliability strategy, current performance, and the historical changes and relevant justifications, is significantly decreased. Coupled with the ability to utilize existing reliability strategy content from similar component types or reliability strategies used on other components of the same type within different areas or plants, ensures an efficient, consistent review, which, in the past, would be a manual exercise in a disparate system that would involve reinventing the wheel.

Leverage key learnings

Digital connected reliability strategies, which form the foundation of the ASMx process, ensure that you know the source of the routine tasks on each asset as it relates back to the corporate baseline reliability strategies. The variations are also recorded and easily visible at all times.

This structure allows for any key learnings or improvements to be implemented locally and instantly assesses deployment to all other assets across the entire asset base that utilize the same baseline reliability strategy, while being mindful of local variations that have been made.

Practically speaking, this also translates to any improvement initiative, which is determined effective for implementation based on a review of a specific component. The improvement can be immediately assessed for all other instances of that component in the same area, on the same site, or all sites within the same country or across an entire global asset base.

With an effective workflow in place, this deployment can be rapid and account for all management of change requirements as part of a reliability strategy change process. In many organizations, their preference may be to just notify asset owners of a recommended change and allow them to assess based on their specific installation of the component/s.

Either way, ASMx provides a vehicle to deploy improvement initiatives and key reliability strategy developments across an entire asset base with a few clicks that, quite simply, isn't possible without it.

SECTION 11

ASM and Reliability Culture

A focus on culture without a framework to support the purpose is likely to lead to feeling good, but achieving little

In simple terms, a culture represents the behaviors and customs of a group of people. A culture is typically shaped by leadership demonstrating what's important to the group and what are acceptable and unacceptable behaviors. Everyone in the group then becomes accustomed to practicing the acceptable behaviors and not doing the unacceptable behaviors, thus reinforcing and further ingraining the culture.

What is a reliability culture?

For many years, it has been professed that our approach to reliability should be like our approach to safety. On the surface, this makes some sense. In safety, the target is zero harm or injuries; in reliability, the target is zero failure or interruptions. Or is it?

The concept is sound and what most people envision is an organization focused on improving reliability the same way they focus on improving safety.

While the notion of driving toward zero failure is not quite technically right, conceptually, the inference is productive. If the whole organization can get on board with the objective of the reliability function and everyone in the organization is educated on the impact they have on performance through equipment reliability or availability, that can only be positive.

This will likely lead to small improvements, predominantly through the reporting of impending equipment issues noted by people outside of the maintenance reliability departments.

The organization may feel better about reliability, but there may not be lasting, step changes in performance. In these typical approaches to reliability culture, what's missing is a framework for the culture to operate in.

The ASM process, when implemented, provides this framework. The process defines what's required from all resources to manage reliability strategies over time and implement improvements.

The impact desired from reliability culture changes is never realized if the actions of the organization don't align to the stated intent. An ASM process ensures the behaviors match the stated intent and reinforce the commitment to reliability through wider organizational involvement and provides a framework for the culture to work within.

Establishing a reliability culture

Establishing a culture or changing an existing one is not an easy task. Some believe culture change can be instantaneous, while others maintain it is a slow, gradual process. Since behaviors can change in an instant and repeated behaviors build culture, perhaps the answer lies somewhere in the middle.

There are several important steps to establishing a culture of reliability:

1. Developing a purpose;
2. Leadership education;

3. Implementing ASM;
4. Reliability education;
5. Process education;
6. Measurement;
7. Communicate, communicate, communicate.

Developing a purpose

What is the purpose of the culture you are trying to build? This needs to be unambiguously stated. It needs to be specific and not general in nature. Targeting zero failures is unlikely to be the real goal, so be clear about what exactly you are trying to achieve.

This is such a critical step; the purpose underpins the whole approach to the cultural change and should drive all the plans and actions taken to affect the cultural change.

It is also a fantastic starting point to engage key stakeholders and other representatives while developing the purpose. If this process is done well, it can support the initial understanding of what you are trying to achieve and the education process begins. Wide-ranging involvement and input also get the word out and start the communication process about the future direction.

Attempting to affect cultural change in the absence of a stated purpose will result in somewhat directionless activities, whereby you may feel you have a culture of reliability, but, ultimately, you are achieving little.

On the flip side, a stated purpose of the reliability culture locks in the direction and provides a reference point for all discussions and decisions. It gives comfort, direction and clarity. For the overwhelming majority, the general human condition drives everyone to do the best they can; a purpose provides the direction so everyone is doing the best they can to achieve a common outcome.

Being such a critical element to the reliability culture journey, organizations may consider engaging an experienced facilitator to work with the group to develop the purpose statement. The investment will pay itself back many times over, simply through the engagement of the team.

Leadership education

It is staggering how many leaders attempt to support or sponsor an initiative without any education, only to later challenge the direction or decisions of those trained. Of course, there is nothing more demoralizing than that, especially for those who invested the time and energy in the education and the effort to make change.

So, leadership education should be the first exercise. Once the purpose is set, it is critical that leadership completely understands the purpose, how it was derived and what it means for the organization.

The basic principles of reliability should be understood and connected to their area of the business. To really support the change, periodic assessments or reviews by the leadership group of the culture movement is worth considering.

Implementing ASM

As stated earlier, implementing ASM ensures a wider framework for reliability improvement is implemented into the organization. It's indicative and supportive of the change and demonstrates the changing focus on reliability and performance.

Section 12 covers in some detail a typical implementation process for ASM.

Reliability education

A program of reliability education should be delivered to the organization. The training program should be role-based and range from one hour overviews to two or three days of intensive learning workshops.

Almost 60% of organizations report that reliability is a stand-alone domain and not connected to other functions of the business

Consistency of education is critical at this stage. The language must be the same and the training needs to connect roles with their influence on reliability.

For the education of the actual reliability practitioners and those significantly involved in the ASM process, it is critical to establish a training program that covers the key aspects to setting a reliability strategy, as covered in an earlier section.

Process education

Once the organization has the required technical understanding of reliability and the culture it is trying to achieve, the next step of process education makes it clear to employees how they contribute from a process perspective.

Given their roles and what the organization is asking of them, how do they participate in the process? How do they raise issues, suggestions, make contributions, get involved, complete and record actions?

Again, if you want to get beyond just feeling great about reliability and make transformational culture change, process is key, as well as people understanding and using the process.

For any process that you want to become part of typical behavior and embed into the business as a usual process, there must be a flow of positive recognition. Simple recognition of involvement in the process that reflects the behaviors you want must be recognized and rewarded.

Measurement

A culture is quite difficult to place a specific measure on, however, some measure of effectiveness is important so the progress can be communicated. In terms of measuring progress toward a culture of reliability, the movement toward the established purpose provides a simple, yet fantastic, indication of the uptake.

Not only is the measurement important, but reporting the progress is key. If the purpose continues to be highly visible with regular measurement and reporting, momentum will be established and a real culture of change will take effect.

Communicate, communicate, communicate

Just like ensuring you have a defined purpose, communication is essential for a successful culture change. Culture is shaped by stating a purpose and rewarding behaviors that move the organization toward the purpose. There's no way you can overcommunicate in this area. The purpose is something that needs constant airtime and discussion. It's not enough to have it written around the place; it needs to be spoken and discussed at every opportunity.

Public recognition of behaviors the organization expects must be discussed regularly and often. The more regular the recognition, the faster the cultural change, providing, of course, the recognition is completely aligned to the behaviors that drive employees to the purpose.

If you have safety shares, perhaps you should consider reliability shares? Keeping the concept front of mind illustrates the importance and the commitment of the organization to performance improvement.

SECTION 12

Implementing ASMx

Implementing ASMx – making it work in your organization

Implementing ASMx into an organization will deliver the best outcomes in the shortest time frame when it is conducted as a dedicated project, with appropriate sponsorship, engagement and resources.

This is not always the case and, in some cases, it is a matter of a single person working in the reliability function promoting the merits of ASM, but facing challenges in getting heard or understood.

Given these possible scenarios, there tends to be two possible paths forward:

1. Get a business case for ASM approved and conduct a full implementation project;
2. Begin applying the key elements of ASM to deliver value and establish support, and then get approval for a full-scale implementation.

With these two options in mind, the following key steps are relevant, but may be completed on different scales. For example, the process calls for rules to be created for packaging tasks into work plans, but they currently don't exist within your organization. Working in isolation, it is still appropriate to develop your own rules, ensure they align to any existing standards that exist and document them. This allows you to begin developing consistency and the rules you develop can be challenged and refined as you establish momentum and support.

In general, a sound implementation project includes, at a minimum, the following steps:

1. Process blueprinting;
2. Technical solution selection;
3. Establish a process;
4. Engagement;
5. Support.

Process blueprinting

Process blueprinting is a critical first step. It is essential to map the existing process used to manage and implement reliability strategy decisions and content, as patchy and disconnected as it may be. This allows all stakeholders to understand the current state and is effective in supporting development of the engagement required to move from the current state to the to-be state.

Once the current process is understood, the to-be state can be developed. The first step is being clear about what the specific objectives of the ASM implementation exactly are. The resource structure needs to be clearly understood so accountabilities can be determined as part of the process definition.

The blueprinting should start with the desired process and then expand to consider roles and responsibilities, required workflows and escalation routes, standard data structures and framework, task packaging rules, reporting required and data flow requirements.

For a complete installation, the blueprinting process typically involves several workshops with key stakeholders who can make decisions regarding review and approval levels and assign owners to specific content.

On the other end of the implementation spectrum, if you are trying to establish ASM with limited support, designing a process of reliability strategy review, approval and implementation will enable the process to start. The key concept to remember is all reliability strategy changes should be made through the ASM process and reviewed by an appropriately educated or experienced subject matter expert.

Technical solution selection

Once the process has been designed, it is time to consider an appropriate technical solution. At a minimum, the technical solution must support the workflow management of reliability strategy changes, including suitable evaluation and justification.

Since the whole concept is to manage the reliability strategy over time, the technical solution should support the creation of an audit log of information as reliability strategies change so, at any point in time, you can review the changes that have occurred to the reliability strategy in the past, by whom, when and the justification.

The technical solution should support the use of generic data sets, wherever possible, while still allowing for specific local variations to reliability strategies. What's key here is that local variations can be made while still maintaining a live link to the generic content.

The technical solution also should support interrogation of the reliability strategy content to determine which generic content is used on a specific asset and which assets generic content has been used on. It should report on all the differences between generic content and actual content based on all the variations that have been made.

For a best in class implementation, the technical solution should have an open architecture to support easy integration into relevant systems, such as the existing EAM system and downtime tracking systems.

To support the triggering of the ASM process, the technical solution should be able to compare forecasted performance against actual performance metrics so areas of disparity can be addressed.

Most importantly, the technical solution should be for an enterprise system that allows for the management of all reliability strategy related content within one environment, with specific user log-ons, security groups and role-based permissions. This supports a single system for storage and management of the reliability strategy content and workflows required to support the ASM process.

For large implementation projects, a technical solution selection is typically formal and looks to satisfy the set technical functional requirements.

For smaller implementations, utilizing an off-site hosted solution to begin the ASM journey is a worthwhile exercise. This will support an efficient ASM process and demonstrate the value and consistency associated with the process.

Establish a process

Any technical solution still requires configuration to match the process as blueprinted. While this should not be a complicated exercise since the ASM technical solution typically supports levels of configuration to ensure alignment to the organization, what's important to keep in mind is a whole process needs to be established.

This requires the establishment of some process steps outside of the ASM technical solution, including integration points and/or changes to some existing processes to lock down the ability to change the reliability strategy content.

In large implementation projects, this step involves detailed process mapping, education, engagement and configuration.

Engagement, of course, will be key to the successful uptake of the ASM process.

Engagement

Engagement is perhaps the most important ingredient in a successful uptake of any new process or change. In terms of ASM, it is usually readily accepted by those within the reliability function since the benefits are clear and the group is motivated to establish a process that supports value delivery to the organization.

The engagement piece is key for those who will be involved in the process, but do not see themselves involved in reliability improvement in the current environment or where the process will mean a reduction in their freedom in terms of manipulating the reliability strategy content directly without any review or approval. Whatever the reason, there will be some personnel who will challenge and resist the change.

Like most implementations, there are four key aspects that should begin the engagement work:

1. Education of the ASM process and the objective of the implementation;
2. Communicating the value and benefits that ASM will bring to the organization;
3. Discussing what is in it for them;
4. Clearly outlining which steps in the process will involve them.

At every stage of this communication plan, allow plenty of time for reflection and questioning by the resources. They will set the scene well for the rest of the implementation.

With the initial communication plan completed, engagement is only just beginning. Continuing to engage relevant resources within the implementation project itself and in the early days of adoption will yield enormous ROI in the time it took to have those conversations.

Involving resources in blueprinting and decision-making allows opportunities to question, learn and contribute, all of which will increase engagement. Working all resources and listening to feedback in the early stages of adoption not only will allow you to rapidly refine the process, but also increase engagement in the process.

Once engagement in the process is established, then longer term, ongoing support can be structured.

Support

The level of support required depends largely on the roles involved and the individuals involved in those roles. However, it is fair to say that support will be required to ensure the process is established as specified and is robust enough to remain in place and become part of business as usual.

As with any project, support will be heavy initially and taper to an ongoing, sustaining level. In the early days, support is about education and on-the-job training and support.

Formal classroom training is the best way to begin the support process. Educate all resources with the appropriate level of detail for their roles within the organization and within the process.

Once the classroom training is complete, regular one-on-one type sessions should be scheduled to encourage questioning and evaluate how the process is being applied. These sessions can then cover adjustments to the process or provide further education in best in class ways to perform certain functions.

Once you are through the initial stages of establishment, support will naturally taper to an organic level of business as usual. Support becomes like any other business process and associated technical solution.

A common trap, however, is not repeating the formal training for any new resources to the organization or the process. Over time, this leads to a drift of expertise within the organization.

A formal education and support plan should be documented and used as an integration plan for any new resources to ensure consistency of approach and rigor around all reliability strategy management processes.

SECTION 13

ASM and New Projects

Using ASMx principles when developing reliability strategies for new projects and new assets means cost-effective delivery of consistent, high quality routine tasks

The build phase of the ASMx process is applicable at the point of developing strategies for new projects or greenfield sites.

Reliability studies for new projects

As a component of most feasibility studies or even at pre-feasibility stage, depending on the project size, it is good practice to develop

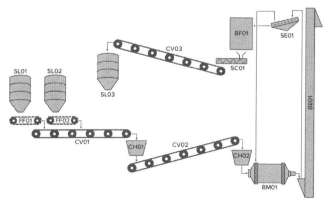

Figure 24: Typical process flow diagram

a reliability block diagram (RBD) simulation model to represent the proposed project.

RBDs are different than process flow diagrams, but new practitioners often confuse the two. Figure 24 shows a typical process flow diagram, in this case for a cement grinding circuit. The process flow diagram, along with an understanding of the system's operations, are used to construct the RBD.

The RBD diagrammatically describes the operational dependencies

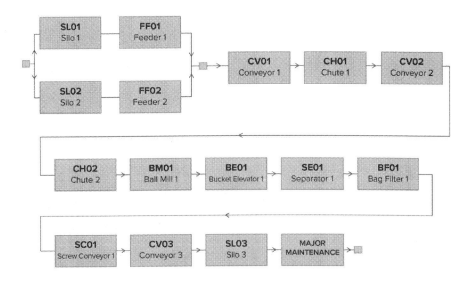

Figure 25: Reliability block diagram of Figure 24

of the project, in other words, areas where single equipment failure takes the project off-line or where there are levels of redundancy.

Once the RBD logic is complete, as in Figure 25, representative data is populated into the RBD to run a simulation and generate a forecast of performance. The obvious question is: Where does the data come from for a new project? The answer lies in your experience with similar assets or components.

In an organization that has implemented ASM, there already is a wealth of indicative reliability strategy and performance related content for most components within the new project.

In an organization where ASM has not been implemented, much of the data probably exists, but not in an easy to understand and ready to use format. It is likely spread across several discrete databases or files.

Either way, the data can be compiled, even if some assumptions must be used that can be reined in as the project progresses, and entered into the RBD diagram.

Typically, a Monte Carlo simulation process is used to simulate the likely performance outcomes using the RBD and the associated data.

Once the RBD model is complete, it can be used to predict performance and evaluate alternative plant, system, or equipment configurations, major maintenance schedules, and plant buffer or surge capacities.

The intent of the model is to support determination of the lowest cost option that will deliver the required performance.

Build a reliability strategy

Once the project moves into the detailed design stage and actual equipment becomes selected, the asset reliability strategies can be developed.

Again, in an organization with ASM implemented, this will be a rapid build through the dynamic assignment of the correct baseline reliability strategy to each actual asset. Local variations then can be made to reflect any specific operational context changes prior to the tasks being packaged automatically into the appropriate master data structures ready for implementation to the EAM system.

In an organization without ASM, the build process is the same, except for an extra step at the beginning to establish the required baseline reliability strategies for the components within the build.

Deploy

The deployment of reliability strategies for new projects typically involves two or three iterations. It is not uncommon for actual assets to change as the project progresses and data becomes available at different stages of the project.

So, once the tasks have been packaged ready for implementation, they are typically loaded into a test stage of the EAM system and run through by appropriate technical resources to check for accuracy and sequencing.

When the plans are run for the first time in the production system, it is good practice to support the technicians and elicit appropriate feedback to make final adjustments to the reliability strategies.

All these iterations should be managed through the same ASM review process as they still constitute a change to the reliability strategy related content.

Do the reliability strategies deliver the performance?

What most reliability strategy development projects miss is any kind of validation that the resulting reliability strategies that are going to be implemented will deliver the required performance.

In most cases, a reliability assessment may be done early in the project's life, but once completed, it is all but forgotten. The reliability strategies are then developed and implemented, and the project goes into the operational phase of its life.

The problem with this, however, is as the project progresses, data becomes more accurate and more detailed. Therefore, it is important to consider the impact of the updated and accurate data on the predicted performance from the reliability block diagram model.

The RBD should be continually updated as the project progresses with updated assumptions, understanding of equipment characteristics, operational philosophies and, of course, the reliability strategies that are to be implemented.

One of the most valuable uses of the RBD is to validate that the reliability strategies, coupled with the final equipment selections and operational philosophies, can deliver the required performance.

There are literally numerous instances where a project received approval based on early reliability modeling, but the model was never updated as the project progresses. This significantly increases the risk that the project, upon completion, will not be capable of delivering the required performance.

Ideally, the RBD is continually updated and, upon completion of the reliability strategy development exercise, used to predict the performance of the project. The model also can be used to predict resource and material requirements and ensure these align to the organizational and procurement plans.

Finally, the RBD model should be handed off to operations to use on an ongoing basis to support debottlenecking studies and the evaluation of improvement options.

SECTION 14

ASM and RCA

If you have separated RCA from reliability strategy, you have missed the opportunity to use history on one asset to change the future of similar assets

Root cause analysis (RCA) is a key aspect of any reliability function. Its aim is to analyze the causes of problems that have occurred and led to undesirable outcomes and implement effective solutions so the problem does not occur again.

It is important to recognize that the goal of any RCA, defect elimination, or problem-solving exercise is not just to understand the causes, but to arrive at effective solution(s).

Typical approaches

As previously stated, it is typical for organizations to separate reliability engineers into two groups: those who are supposed to review reliability strategy and those trained to perform RCA investigations.

There are two key problems with this approach:

1. Some events will trigger an RCA investigation, when, in fact, it is very clearly a reliability strategy review exercise that should be completed;

2. In many cases in equipment related RCAs, there will be some solutions associated with changing the reliability strategy.

What occurs is very little connection between any reliability strategy work and RCA work. Even in instances where RCA solutions involve a reliability strategy update, they are usually completed based on subject matter expert opinion and are not subjected to any kind of reliability strategy review decision framework, review and justification.

Probably the biggest limitation with having a disconnected RCA and reliability strategy review process is the inability to leverage learnings and good solutions across the entire asset base.

What is seen in most organizations is a real challenge to translate what are excellent solutions generated during an RCA for a specific asset failure to all relevant installations of that asset across the entire organization.

Incorporating RCA into ASM

This translation issue is the main driver behind incorporating RCA into the ASM process and, specifically, to an ASMx implementation.

In an ASMx implementation, it is understood exactly what component type each asset is and where all the similar components are located, so there is a very clear digital path to translate any key learnings or improvements.

In fact, if an RCA is completed on a specific asset, the RCA leader can connect that investigation or solution to that specific asset in the ASMx asset hierarchy. From there, it can be determined which generic component that asset is connected to and where else that component is used.

This process can become part of the workflow so that appropriate resources are notified that an RCA has been completed and to review for relevant updates regionally or globally and notify the specific asset owners of an update that can be made to the assets or reliability strategies.

The other benefit is if an RCA determines there is a need for a reliability strategy change, this change will go through the normal ASM reliability strategy review, approve and justification workflow, ensuring consistent and sound reliability strategy decisions.

The implementation path is also clear and efficient, ensuring that updates occur in the EAM system.

ASM specialists

Since RCA is being incorporated into the ASM process, all reliability engineers should be educated on the key concepts of the reliability strategy review and RCA investigations.

This ability to conduct sound RCAs and complete a reliability strategy review to an appropriate level of detail not only improves productivity, but also the quality of the improvement initiatives.

Having both techniques part of the same process and framework makes enormous sense because all reliability engineers will be working within one technical system for all reliability work.

Having reliability engineers focus on both RCA and strategy also has the benefit of supporting appropriate triggers. When a trigger is reached and a review is required, the associated reliability engineer can use his or her skills to support the determination of whether the review should incorporate an RCA or be a pure reliability strategy review. While it is not critical since each technique can be used at any time, there is no direct science as to which methodology to start with, but rather some guiding principles that can be used.

The capabilities of reliability engineers would develop in such a way that they would clearly recognize when to switch between RCA and strategy, or when the process they are following is the appropriate approach.

While it might sound complex for a reliability engineer to specialize in both RCA and strategy, this is simply not the case. The theoretical content for both is not complex and simply requires practice with a certain amount of initial support. It typically fails because people learn the theoretical content, but then there is no framework to operate in or triggers to drive the application.

So, with the implementation of ASM, ASM specialists will develop their expertise with capabilities in all aspects of RCA and reliability strategy development, review and optimization.

SECTION 15

ASMx Quick Start

To deliver real value, it's got to work in your organization

This section serves as a stand-alone segment designed to outline the minimum foundational elements to support a quick start implementation of ASMx. This quick start serves organizations that have some elements already implemented, as well as those starting from a zero base with no formal ASM.

These minimum elements must be considered and implemented to classify the ASM process as a full implementation that will deliver value on an ongoing basis.

The contents of this section assume a certain level of asset management and reliability expertise. The preceding sections cover the elements in more detail for those who need in-depth information.

The information is presented in bullet point format to keep it short and concise.

The section covers the minimum foundational items of:

1. Key elements of a reliability strategy build/review;
2. Baseline reliability strategies;

3. Initial deployment to assets;
4. Implementing a reliability strategy;
5. ASMx triggers;
6. ASMx technology;
7. ASMx implementation on mature sites.

Key elements of a reliability strategy build/review

1. Functional approach – Ensure routine tasks are designed to support the required function, either through functional analysis or detailed effects of failure quantification.
2. Use Weibull analysis to describe failure characteristics – While it doesn't have to be Weibull, it is the simplest distribution to use for equipment failure characteristics. You must use a distribution capable of describing change failure rates over time.
3. Ensure key resources understand the distinction between preventive and predictive tasks.
4. Ensure key resources understand the P-F interval.
5. Ensure key resources understand that online monitoring is a form of a predictive task, just a continuous one.
6. Classify each routine task as either a preventive task or a predictive tasks – These are the only task types there are.
7. Quantify the effects of failure and align them to any existing risk management framework.
8. Use a qualitative analysis to compare and determine the optimal task for each failure mode.

Baseline reliability strategies

1. Develop a baseline FMECA for each component type. This content should be used for all instances of that component type so there is no duplication. This will minimize the amount of FMECA work required.

2. Generate reliability strategy overrides for component types implemented in different criticalities or operating contexts. This means using the same base FMECA data, but just describing modifications to failure characteristics, task intervals and enablement based on different criticality or operating context installations of the component.
3. Generate make/model overrides for the materials used within the tasks. This allows the specification of certain materials with, for example, catalog material numbers, for specific make/models of the component.
4. Use consistent structures for failure mode descriptions and task descriptions. Ideally, use phrase libraries.
5. Specify acceptable limits/desirable outcomes for each task.
6. As a general rule, ensure each failure mode represents only one failure mechanism and cause of failure.
7. Build code groups aligned to what's used in the EAM system and assign codes to each failure mode.
8. As a general rule, ensure each failure model has one task.
9. It's okay to have one task description that covers several failure modes duplicated across the relevant failure modes. This supports a better quality task instruction document at implementation.

Initial deployment to assets

1. Ensure you understand what type of equipment each asset is or is made up of (i.e., what component or components is it comprised of?). For example, if the asset is a pump, what type of pump is it? A reciprocating positive displacement pump and a centrifugal pump have very different failure modes and causes.
2. Ensure criticality is understood for each asset. Given the operating context and environment, how critical is the asset to the organization's operational goals? The same asset type installed in locations with different criticalities may call for different reliability strategies.

3. Ideally, understand make/model information for each asset.
4. Connect the baseline content for the relevant component to all relevant assets.
5. Make any required local variations to align the generic content to the operational context of each actual asset.
6. This process should be done while still maintaining the connection to the baseline reliability strategies.

Implementing a reliability strategy

1. Develop task packaging rules. These rules should document the decision-making process to follow. The rules describe how to group a list of tasks on a collection of assets into the required master data structures for implementation to the EAM system.
2. It is okay to have multiple packaging structures. For example, mobile assets may have a different packaging structure to fixed plant assets. This simply means the first decision in the rule engine is associated with which type of asset is being packaged.
3. Very clear data standards should be established and implemented.
4. Ideally, the packaging process is completely automatic and doesn't require any manual modifications or overrides. This ensures compliance to the standards and the business rules.
5. Electronic integration is best and most efficient. Its development is worth the investment. If there is any step in the process involving spreadsheets or manual translation or manipulation, there is room for error.

ASMx triggers

1. Triggers are essential to ensure the process of improvement continues. In the absence of leading triggers, the process will be triggered only when undesirable events have already occurred. This is being performance led.

2. Triggers should cover the occurrence of any change that would drive a reliability strategy review:
   a. Change in market conditions, resulting in changes to the cost impact of failures;
   b. Change in operating conditions or environment;
   c. Change in performance of the asset:
      i. Increasing life;
      ii. Decreasing life;
      iii. Change in forecasted planned hours;
      iv. Change in forecasted costs;
      v. Predictive technology changes.
3. Ideally, triggers are automatic. Using real data review triggers can be automatic and create notifications to the responsible personnel.

ASMx technology

The ASMx technology should:

1. Support management of generic content at several levels:
   a. Corporate;
   b. Region;
   c. Site.
2. Support quantitative financial and risk optimization of routine maintenance;
3. Have dynamic assignment of the generic content to actual assets based on criticality, operating context and make/model;
4. Allow for variations at all levels while maintaining connection to the generic content;
5. Promote rule-based task packaging into structured master data;
6. Integrate into EAM systems;
7. Incorporate RCA and the ability to link investigations to actual assets and component types;
8. Promote a configurable workflow and notification engine

to support ASM process flows with associated review and approval steps.

ASMx implementation on mature sites

The process of implementation should follow a standard path for brownfield sites or any site where reliability strategies are being redeveloped, optimized and implemented into the system as if it is a new system.

Typical implementation steps are covered in an earlier section. However, in terms of reliability strategy content, the implementation steps should be:

1. Develop baseline reliability strategies for all components, criticalities and makes/models required. For most mature organizations, this involves using an existing maintenance plan and any legacy reliability analysis data available.
2. Connect baseline reliability strategies to the asset hierarchy.
3. Make local variations.
4. Package the tasks into maintenance plans.
5. Implement into the EAM system.
6. Set triggers and begin the reliability strategy management process.

It is best to complete a full implementation, however, this may not be practical. It may make sense to only review assets performing poorly.

The other consideration is sites where current plans will not be completely turned off and new plans loaded. In this case, a different style of implementation may be applicable:

1. Ensure the asset hierarchy is complete, along with criticality assessment and make/model designation.
2. Identify components required to complete the analysis.
3. Create components required if there is any legacy reliability analysis work available.
4. Where applicable, connect components to the actual assets.

5. Define and implement packaging rules, but do not package tasks at this stage.
6. Define and implement triggers.
7. Monitor and review either the reliability strategies based on the triggers or a defined project, such as all critical assets. This means as the reviews are completed, any component data required will be built and become part of the ASM system.
8. The process of review is:
    a. Import the current plans by creating an "as-is" scenario and attaching all current tasks to the listed failure modes.
    b. Where there are no existing components, create a baseline reliability strategy.
    c. Review and optimize the reliability strategy.
        i. Be careful when selecting the boundaries around the study set. They should be consistent with the maintenance plan structures in the EAM system so that complete plans, not partial ones, can be updated.
    d. Use the previously configured packaging rules to generate new package structures.
    e. Generate and implement the changes required to the existing plans to reflect the new optimized reliability strategies.

The goal of this process is twofold:
1. Allows the review process to drive the completion of the reliability strategy content over time. This ensures that effort is spent where it adds the most value.
2. Makes use of already mature reliability strategies to drive continuous improvement.

In every case, a specific implementation plan should be developed and aligned to the organization, its structure, asset management maturity, resources and appetite for improvement or risk management.

SECTION 16

ASMx – Manage Reliability Strategy & Drive Performance

Transforming an organization from being performance led to driving performance puts you back in control

This book has addressed a major flaw in most organizations' asset management systems. There is no process in place to ensure that the reliability strategies and resulting detailed routine maintenance and corrective action plans are current, complete, accurate and aligned to the operating environment of the day.

Setting a reliability strategy has been a project activity completed for new assets, when a new EAM system is being implemented, or perhaps, on single problematic assets.

It is understood by most that how you care for and maintain an asset is fundamentally connected to the performance you will get from that asset and, in many cases, is one of the biggest influences of that performance.

With that in mind, it is quite staggering to consider that the asset management discipline has evolved in such a way that there is limited focus on ensuring the fundamental driver of the resulting asset performance is managed over time.

There has been enormous focus on WEM, perhaps largely driven by the proliferation of technical solutions and the perception of control of asset performance that has manifested. This misleading belief is the reason many EAM system implementations have failed to deliver the benefits that were targeted.

More recently, APM has been a point of focus based on a desire to connect data to reliability. What's most misunderstood here is that monitoring performance leads to a reactive cycle of attempted improvements, as these are typically focused on single assets.

This book has demonstrated how ASM works with the WEM and APM processes to allow an organization to gain control of assets and begin to drive performance outcomes. ASM is an ongoing process that is focused on ensuring that the reliability strategies and resulting routine maintenance tasks in place are always aligned to the performance goals and based on current knowledge, data and operating environment.

ASMx delivers ASM in a digitally connected environment, supporting the leverage of knowledge and data-driven insight across the entire asset base and improving productivity and efficiency with consistent, complete data.

It all starts with strategy! Implementing ASM first will deliver the most rapid improvements. ASM generates the master data required for WEM and supports the development of the required APM. Implementing ASM, coupled with the foundations of a reliability culture and leadership, will transform an organization's approach to asset reliability and will result in a step change in asset performance.

References

Abernethy, Robert B. *The New Weibull Handbook*. Robert B. Abernethy, 1993.

Barringer, H. Paul. *How To Use Reliability Engineering Principles For Business Issues*. Barringer & Associates, Inc., 1998, pp. 1–22, *How To Use Reliability Engineering Principles For Business Issues*.

Moubray, John. *Reliability-Centered Maintenance*. Industrial Press, 1997.

O'Hanlon, Terrence, and Ramesh Gulati. *10 Rights of Asset Management*. Reliabilityweb.com, 2017.

About the Author

As the pioneer of asset strategy management, a process enabled by people, data and technology to sustain a reliability-driven approach to improving asset performance, Jason Apps has evolved his approach to reliability improvement over a twenty year consulting career.

In his current role as CEO of ARMS Reliability, Jason recognizes that a purpose-driven company enables a strong, sustainable, scalable organizational culture. He has been instrumental in developing ARMS Reliability's values and mission statement and infusing its purpose in everything the company does.

Jason oversees all of ARMS Reliability's global operations, focused on helping its clients be safe and successful by making reliability a reality.

While studying mechanical engineering at Swinburne University of Technology, Jason served as a cadet engineer at Alcoa, where he later took up maintenance reliability engineering roles.

About the Author

Jason joined ARMS Reliability in 1998 and began his reliability consulting career. Over the course of time and many successful reliability projects later, a trend was apparent. Clients were spending time and money to improve their asset performance, but these new and improved reliability strategies were not being implemented and/or sustained. In his role as Technical Director, Jason set out to understand why this was happening and develop a solution.

Jason became CEO of ARMS Reliability in 2016 and led the development of the asset strategy management process and ARMS Reliability's technical ASM solution, OnePM. Jason continues to evolve ARMS Reliability's approach to developing, implementing and monitoring asset-based reliability strategies and manage them all through a centralized digital reliability strategy platform. The focus is on reliability strategies that continually evolve based on data-driven analytics to deliver the optimal balance of cost, risk and performance.

Jason is passionate about the value ASM can deliver and feels fortunate and privileged to lead a team of extremely motivated and talented individuals who continue to innovate and focus on solving customers' challenges.

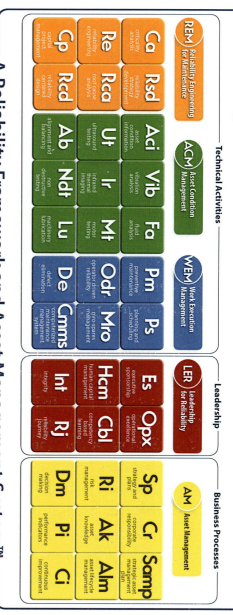

ABOUT RELIABILITYWEB.COM

Created in 1999, Reliabilityweb.com provides educational information and peer-to-peer networking opportunities that enable safe and effective reliability and asset management for organizations around the world.

ACTIVITIES INCLUDE:

Reliabilityweb.com® (www.reliabilityweb.com) includes educational articles, tips, video presentations, an industry event calendar and industry news. Updates are available through free email subscriptions and RSS feeds. **Confiabilidad.net** is a mirror site that is available in Spanish at www.confiabilidad.net.

Uptime® Magazine (www.uptimemagazine.com) is a bi-monthly magazine launched in 2005 that is highly prized by the reliability and asset management community. Editions are obtainable in both print and digital.

Reliability Leadership Institute® Conferences and Training Events (www.reliabilityleadership.com) offer events that range from unique, focused-training workshops and seminars to large focused conferences to industry-wide events, including the International Maintenance Conference (IMC), MaximoWorld and The RELIABILITY Conference™ (TRC).

MRO-Zone Bookstore (www.mro-zone.com) is an online bookstore offering a reliability and asset management focused library of books, DVDs and CDs published by Reliabilityweb.com.

Association of Asset Management Professionals (www.maintenance.org) is a member organization and online community that encourages professional development and certification and supports information exchange and learning with 50,000+ members worldwide.

A Word About Social Good

Reliabilityweb.com is mission-driven to deliver value and social good to the reliability and asset management communities. *Doing good work and making profit is not inconsistent*, and as a result of Reliabilityweb.com's mission-driven focus, financial stability and success has been the outcome. For over a decade, Reliabilityweb.com's positive contributions and commitment to the reliability and asset management communities have been unmatched.

Other Causes

Reliabilityweb.com has financially contributed to include industry associations, such as SMRP, AFE, STLE, ASME and ASTM, and community charities, including the Salvation Army, American Red Cross, Wounded Warrior Project, Paralyzed Veterans of America and the Autism Society of America. In addition, we are proud supporters of our U.S. Troops and first responders who protect our freedoms and way of life. That is only possible by being a for-profit company that pays taxes.

I hope you will get involved with and explore the many resources that are available to you through the Reliabilityweb.com network.

Warmest regards,
Terrence O'Hanlon
CEO, Reliabilityweb.com

Reliabilityweb.com®, Uptime®, The RELIABILITY Conference™, MaximoWorld and Reliability Leadership Institute® are the trademarks or registered trademarks of Reliabilityweb.com and its affiliates in the USA and in several other countries.